More American Dolls From the Post-War Era
1945 - 1965

Cynthia Gaskill

Gold Horse Publishing
Annapolis, Maryland

Copyright©1993. All rights reserved. No parts of this book may be reproduced inany form without the permission, in writing, of the author and the publisher.

For inquiries regarding additional copies contact Gold Horse Publishing, a division of Dollmaster's, P.O. Box 2319, Annapolis, Maryland 21404 or call 800-966-3655.

Cover design and art direction by Susan Robinson
Photography by Robert Bartlett.

Printed in Hong Kong
ISBN 0-912823-43-7.
Gold Horse Publishing
Annapolis, Maryland

Introduction

The dolls within this book were created within the 20-year period of 1945-1965 that can be considered the Golden Age of doll-making in America. It was a similar phenomena to the Golden Age of doll-making that existed in France between 1870-1890 when giants such as Emile Jumeau and Casimir Bru created their masterpieces. During each of these eras experimental molds were designed, new mediums were used and masterpieces were created. Some dolls were an immediate success and sold thousands, others more controversial or avant-garde or more expensive in production or simply less available for a myriad of reasons are now today's treasures, prized for their rarity.

The dates change but the result is the same. One era in each century stands alone as a moment of time in its creativity and ingenuousness.

In the 20th century this was the post-war period from 1945-1965. During this time new plastic formulas were being discovered and the mass-production retail doll industry was in its infancy. Couture doll fashions were copied from Paris originals and scaled accordingly including a full range of accessories. Madame Alexander, now a household name, was winning fashion awards for her costume designs with the dolls they graced, award winners in their own right. She captured every girl's fantasies with her creations wrapped in yards of satin, taffeta and tulle decorated with rhinestones and floral garlands.

And a teen-ager named Barbie was brought on the market, cloned from the German Bild-Lilli doll; she had her own fabulous tailored fashions, friends and over time every conceivable accessory. A retail flop at first, when she finally did come of age, she never once looked back.

The mid 60's brought about social changes that would forever alter the doll industry. Increases in production meant decreases in quality and time or money wasn't afforded to create the master pieces of the post-war years which were, indeed, the Golden Age of modern dolls as these legendary examples within will attest.

1. IDEAL 'BETSY WETSY' IN LAYETTE

14". Hard plastic head, sleep eyes, pierced nostrils and tear ducts, open mouth for bottle, fleeced light-brown hair, five-piece vinyl body. Original striped dress, bonnet, wrist tag and faux alligator suitcase with layette. Circa 1950. Marked 14 Ideal Doll, Made in the U.S.A.

2. BELLE CHARACTER BABY

14". Vinyl head, sleep eyes, closed mouth, molded hair, one-piece soft rubber body. Original organdy dress with matching knit sweater and hat, original box with 'Belle' label. Circa 1955. Marked 'MRP'.

3. HORSMAN'S 'DRAFT DODGER BABY DOLL'

14". Vinyl head, sleep eyes, closed mouth, molded hair, one-piece, soft vinyl fairy skin body. Original red and white striped flannel 'Draft Dodger Garment' with sleeping cap and booties, original wrist tag. Packaged in original red Horsman 'Art Doll' box. Circa 1956. Marked BC 2/Horsman.

4. EUGENE CHARACTER BABY

14". Vinyl head, glassine sleep eyes, closed mouth, molded hair, one-piece soft rubber body. Original christening gown, bonnet and socks. Original price tag attached to gown. Packaged in Eugene Doll and Novelty Co., NY box. Circa 1955. Marked MRP.

5. ALLIED CHARACTER BABY

16". Vinyl head, sleep eyes, closed mouth, molded hair, one-piece, soft rubber body. Original embossed cotton chintz dress and bonnet, original Allied Quality Doll tag. Original pink Allied-Grand Doll Co., Brooklyn, NY box. Circa 1955. No marks.

6. AMERICAN CHARACTER 'SWEET SUE' WALKING DOLL

30". Hard plastic head with rich facial coloring, sleep eyes, closed mouth, blonde, saran, short hair, jointed vinyl and hard plastic body. Original blue nylon dress with lace and flowers, straw hat with flower, and straw purse. Blue and white American Character logo box. Circa 1955. Marked American Character on head.

7. GRANT 'SUZY' TODDLER DOLL

10". Vinyl plastic head, sleep eyes, closed mouth, rooted blonde hair, jointed hard plastic body with bendable knees. One of many 'dress-me-dolls' available, she wears only panties, socks and shoes, original multi-color box. Circa 1960. Marked Eegee.

8. GRANT 'SUZY' COMPANION TODDLER DOLL

10". Vinyl plastic head, sleep eyes, closed mouth, rooted brown hair, five-piece hard plastic body with bendable knees. Original box included. Circa 1960. Marked Eegee.

9. TWO SUZY FASHIONS

Includes blue and white print, two-piece pajama and pink and black ice set with silver skates. Both mint in original packages.

10. SUZY BRIDAL GOWN FASHION

White satin gown with tulle veil, panties, bouquet, garter and shoes included. Mint in original package.

11. TWO SUZY FASHIONS

Includes red and white print, two-piece pajama and yellow and black ice set with silver skates. Mint in original packages.

12. IDEAL 'MISS CURITY' NURSE DOLL

14". Hard plastic head, sleep eyes with smoky shadow, closed mouth, blonde washable hair with net, five-piece hard plastic child body. Wearing original cotton nurse's uniform, cap and cape. Original curlers on tag, original labeled box. Circa 1953. Marked P90 Ideal Doll, Made in USA.

13. IDEAL 'MISS CURITY' NURSE DOLL

14". Hard plastic head, sleep eyes with smoky shadow, closed mouth, blonde washable hair with net, five-piece hard plastic body. Wearing original cotton nurse's uniform, cap and cape. Original curlers on tag, original labeled box (some wear) and 'Play Nurse Kit' bag with supplies. Circa 1953. Marked P90 Ideal Doll, Made in USA.

14. EEGEE 'LITTLE DEBUTANTE' FASHION DOLL

16". Vinyl head, bright blue sleep eyes, closed mouth, rooted auburn hair, pierced ears, soft vinyl, bendable body. Original pink party dress with tulle petticoat, floral sash and hat, pink open-toe heels. Mint original wrist tag and box. Circa 1958. Marked Eegee/H15.

15. EEGEE 'LITTLE DEBUTANTE' FASHION DOLL

16". Vinyl head, bright blue sleep eyes, closed mouth, rooted blonde hair, pierced ears, soft vinyl, poseable body. Original black velvet and white blouse outfit, straw hat and black, open-toe heels. Mint original wrist tag and box. Circa 1958. Marked Eegee/H15.

16. WALKER DOLL ATTRIBUTED TO ROBERTA

19". Hard plastic head, sleep eyes, open mouth with four teeth, brown hair, five-piece child body. Printed cotton dress, pearls, shoes and socks. Circa 1955. Marked 210.

17. ROBERTA WALKER DOLL

16". Hard plastic head, sleep eyes, open mouth with four teeth, blonde hair, five-piece hard plastic child body. Original wrist tag, blue and white cotton play dress with attached panties. Appears to bear the likeness and marks of 'Cindy' by Horsman which is not unusual as much interaction occurred during this time period among a number of firms. Circa 1955. Marked 170/Made in USA.

18. IDEAL 'SAUCY WALKER' DOLL

22". Vinyl head, sleep eyes, closed mouth, brown hair, five-piece hard plastic child body. Original printed cotton dress under blue button-up coat and hat, wrist tag with curlers, extra pair of shoes, original box. Circa 1952. Marked Ideal SW/Made in USA.

19. TERRI LEE WITH BOX

16". Hard plastic head, painted facial features, brown curled hair, five-piece hard plastic child body. Original tagged red taffeta "Sunday School Dress", white socks and shoes, pink ruffled panties, original hair net. Original yellow box with 'Fashion Centers' booklet. Circa 1952. Marked Terri Lee on back.

20. TINY JERRI LEE WALKER IN BOX

10". Hard plastic head, brown sleep eyes with lashes, brown lambswool wig, five-piece hard plastic child body. Original tagged red & white checked blouse with denim pants, white socks and shoes. Original red box with white bow and friendship club membership card. Circa 1956. Marked c (in circle) on back.

21. TINY TERRI LEE WALKER

10". Hard plastic head, brown sleep eyes with lashes, light-brown curls, five-piece hard plastic child body. Original tagged 'Ice Skater' costume (no skates). Tiny Terri Lee booklet included. Circa 1956. Marked c (in circle) on back.

22. TERRI LEE IN ORIGINAL BOX

16". Hard plastic head, painted facial features, brown curls, five-piece hard plastic child body. Original western shirt, jeans, boots and felt cowboy hat. Original red bow box includes original pamphlets. Circa 1952. Marked Terri Lee on back.

23. LINDA LEE BABY SISTER

9". Vinyl head with painted features, molded hair, five-piece vinyl baby body. White cotton dress and tagged slip, cotton diapers. Circa 1951. Includes birth certificate, hospital admission card, brochure and box end flap.

24. TERRI LEE BRIDE AND JERRI LEE GROOM

16". Both dolls with hard plastic heads, painted features, five-piece child body. Jerri Lee with white lambswool wig, Terri Lee in blonde curls. Tagged outfits include white satin and net dress with floral accents, net veil with rose garland and bouquet, and white rayon shirt with black satin tie, two-piece white cotton suit, blue striped boxers. Circa 1952. Both marked Terri Lee.

25. FREYDBERG'S MARY JANE WALKER

17". Hard plastic head with green sleep/flirty eyes, molded lashes, five-piece child body, black wiry wig. Dressed in net blouse, slip and multi-print jumper. Circa 1953. No marks. This doll, a product of GH & E Freydberg Inc. of New York, was the Terri Lee imitator that caused a lawsuit to be brought against Freydberg claiming patent infringement. All remaining dolls were to be destroyed by the manufacturer in 1954.

26. GROUP OF ASSORTED TERRI LEE BOOKLETS

Includes Terri Lee Magazine-September 1957, Fashion Parade booklet, Terri Lee Family booklet, Connie Lynn pamphlet and doll hospital admission card.

27. RITZI CHUBBY BABY DOLL

13". Vinyl head, inset plastic eyes with painted whites, closed mouth, one-piece soft rubber baby body. All original, mint condition with box and tag. Circa 1955. No marks.

28. RITZI CHUBBY TODDLER

16". Vinyl head, sleep eyes, closed mouth, molded hair, one-piece soft rubber toddler body. Dressed in shirt, pants and saddle shoes with original tag. Circa 1955. Number 4364 on head.

29. EFFANBEE MICKEY THE ALL-AMERICAN BOY

11". Vinyl head, painted features includes freckles, closed mouth, molded hair and baseball cap, five-piece vinyl child body. Wearing red and white striped baseball uniform, socks and shoes. All-original mint condition in original box with plastic baseball. Circa 1960. Marked c (in circle) F & B on back.

30. EFFANBEE PATSY ANN GIRL SCOUT

15". Vinyl head, sleep eyes, closed mouth, freckles, brown rooted hair, five-piece hard vinyl child body. Wears green Girl Scout uniform with tie, beret, belt and panties. Original wrist tag. Circa 1959. Marked Effanbee Patsy Ann c 1959 on head/Effanbee on back.

31. EFFANBEE PATSY ANN BROWNIE

15". Vinyl head, blue sleep eyes, closed mouth, freckles, brown rooted hair, five-piece hard vinyl child body. Wears Brownie uniform with hat, belt and panties. Circa 1959. Marked Effanbee Patsy Ann c 1959 on head/Effanbee on back.

32. EFFANBEE PATSY ANN GIRL SCOUT

15". Vinyl head, sleep eyes, closed mouth, freckles, blonde rooted hair, five-piece hard vinyl child body. Wears green Girl Scout uniform with tie, beret, belt and panties. Original wrist tag. Circa 1959. Marked Effanbee Patsy Ann c 1959 on head/Effanbee on back.

33. EFFANBEE PATSY ANN BROWNIE

15". Vinyl head, sleep eyes, closed mouth, freckles, blonde rooted hair, five-piece hard vinyl child body. Wears Brownie uniform with hat, belt, and panties. Original wrist tag. Circa 1959. Marked Effanbee Patsy Ann c 1959 on head/Effanbee on back.

34. IDEAL MARY HARTLINE
16". Hard plastic head, sleep eyes with smoky shadow, closed mouth, blonde hair, five-piece hard plastic child body. Wears blue drum majorette costume and white/red boots. Circa 1952. Marked Ideal Doll Made in USA on head/Ideal Doll P-91 on back. Also included is a Rand McNally Elf Book "Super Circus" featuring Mary Hartline.

35. TINY IDEAL MARY HARTLINE
7 1/2". Hard shiny plastic, sleep eyes, closed mouth, blonde hair, three-piece child body. Red majorette dress with painted boots. Includes wooden baton with gold ball tip. Circa 1952 catalogue, #1250. Marked Ideal on back.

36. IDEAL MARY HARTLINE
16". Hard plastic head, sleep eyes with smoky shadow, closed mouth, blonde hair, five-piece child body. Red v-neck majorette dress with boots. Original wrist tag and baton. Includes promotional picture. Circa 1952. Marked Ideal Doll Made in USA on head/Ideal Doll P-91 on back.

37. AMERICAN CHARACTER SWEET SUE WALKER
24". Hard plastic head which turns from side to side as she walks, sleep eyes, closed mouth, curled blonde hair, five-piece child body. Original coral nylon dress with organdy sleeves and inset floral bonnet. Circa 1952. Marked American Character on head.

38. AMERICAN CHARACTER SWEET SUE WALKER
24". Hard plastic head which turns from side to side as she walks, sleep eyes, closed mouth, curled blonde hair, hard plastic torso and jointed legs, vinyl jointed arms. Original 'American Beauty' pink satin gown with tulle accents and overskirt, applied blue roses, hoop underskirt. Circa 1952. Marked Amer Char Doll on head.

39. IDEAL BETSY WETSY IN ORIGINAL LAYETTE

12". Vinyl head with sleep eyes, open mouth for bottle, rooted ash-blonde hair, five-piece vinyl baby body. Original mint condition with wrist tag, instructions and layette in multi-colored box with ribbon design on top. Circa 1960. Marked Ideal Doll VW-1 on head.

40. MADAME ALEXANDER 'JANIE'

12". Vinyl head, grey sleep eyes, closed mouth, pug nose, rooted brown hair, five-piece plastic child body. Original tagged red and white school dress with hanging pencil/arithmetic book, wrist tag and box. Circa 1964. Marked Alexander 19c64 on head.

41. BLOCK BABY WALKER

10". Hard plastic head that turns when walking, sleep eyes, closed mouth, brown hair, five-piece hard plastic toddler body with vivid coloring. Mint in original decorated box with lilac nylon panties. Circa 1954. Made by the Block Doll Corp. of New York.

42. BLOCK BABY WALKER

10". Hard plastic head that turns when walking, sleep eyes, closed mouth, brown hair, five-piece hard plastic toddler body with vivid coloring. Mint in original decorated box with light-blue nylon panties. Circa 1954. Block Dolls mass-produced smaller, less expensive quality dolls for the market.

43. IDEAL SHIRLEY TEMPLE IN BOX

19". Soft vinyl head, sleep eyes, open mouth with six teeth, dimples, rooted curly blonde locks, high cheek color, five-piece hard vinyl child body. Original tagged yellow rayon dress with white nylon pinafore, silver name pin, plastic white clutch, wrist tag, original pink box (no lid). Circa 1957. Marked ST-19-1 on head, Ideal Doll ST-19 on back.

44. IDEAL SHIRLEY TEMPLE IN BLUE JUMPER

12". Vinyl head, sleep eyes, smiling open mouth with teeth, rooted curly blonde hair, five-piece hard vinyl child body. Original tagged blue velvet jumper outfit with pink slip and panties, white clutch, original wrist tag, orange and white box. Circa 1958. Marked Ideal Doll ST-12. Comes with extra tagged two-piece blue Navy outfit with cap, red tie, shoes, and panties.

45. IDEAL SHIRLEY TEMPLE IN PLAID DRESS

12". Vinyl head, sleep eyes, smiling open mouth with teeth, rooted curly blonde hair, five-piece hard vinyl child body. Red and green plaid dress with attached red sash, pink slip and panties, red purse. Circa 1958. Marked Ideal Doll ST-12.

46. IDEAL SHIRLEY TEMPLE IN PINK SLIP

12". Vinyl head, sleep eyes, smiling open mouth with teeth, rooted curly blonde hair, five-piece hard vinyl child body. Tagged pink nylon slip and panties, original white box with gold stars. Circa 1958-59. Marked Ideal Doll ST-12.

47. IDEAL SHIRLEY TEMPLE IN SAILOR DRESS

15". Vinyl head, sleep eyes, smiling open mouth with teeth, rooted curly blonde hair, five-piece hard vinyl child body. Tagged blue, white and red sailor dress with silver name pin and beret. Circa 1957. Marked Ideal Doll ST-15-N.

48. MADAME ALEXANDER 'MARGOT' BALLERINA

14". Hard plastic head which turns when walking, sleep eyes, closed mouth, blonde wig with hair net intact, five-piece hard plastic child body. Tagged pink satin and tulle tutu with rhinestone accents, net stockings, ballet shoes and pink hatbox with curlers, booklet and fashion academy medal. Circa 1954. Pristine condition with original box.

49. MADAME ALEXANDER 'MARGOT' BALLERINA

14". Hard plastic head which turns when walking, sleep eyes, closed mouth, auburn hair with net, five-piece hard plastic child body. Tagged pink satin and tulle tutu with rhinestone accents, net stockings, ballet shoes and pink hatbox with curlers, booklet and fashion academy medal. Circa 1954. Remarkable facial coloring is enhanced by rarer auburn hair coloring.

50. MADAME ALEXANDER 'CYNTHIA'

17". Hard plastic head, sleep eyes, closed mouth, black hair, five-piece hard plastic child body. Tagged 'Cynthia', mint-colored organdy dress with lace accents, straw bonnet with flowers and satin ribbons. Circa 1952-53. Faintest ALEX on head.

51. MADAME ALEXANDER 'CYNTHIA'

14". Hard plastic head, sleep eyes, closed mouth, black hair tied with yellow ribbon, five-piece hard plastic child body. Tagged 'Madame Alexander', yellow organdy dress with lace ruffles. Circa 1952-3. Note the gentle facial blushing.

52. MADAME ALEXANDER 'McGUFFEY ANA'

14". Hard plastic Margaret head, sleep eyes, closed mouth, honey-blonde mohair wig, curls in front, five-piece hard plastic child body. Original tagged two-piece outfit (blue cotton dress topped by floral print pinafore) with cotton slip and underpants with blue bows, white stockings, black ankle boots and straw bonnet. Original clover name tag. Circa 1948. Marked ALEX on head.

53. MADAME ALEXANDER 'SNOW WHITE'

8". Hard plastic head, sleep eyes, closed mouth, brown curled hair, five-piece hard plastic child body. Tagged blue velvet bodice over yellow skirt, ruffled underskirt all covered by a scarlet cape with silver and white enlarged collar. Original wrist booklet. Circa 1972-76. Marked ALEX on back. A limited production made only for Disneyland/World.

54. AMERICAN CHARACTER 'I LOVE LUCY BABY'

14". Hard plastic head, sleep eyes, open mouth, molded hair, five-piece rubber baby body. Pink nylon playsuit with felt appliques, robe and bonnet with ruffles, pink knitted booties. Original box opens to reveal "quilted" lining with pull-out drawer containing extra diaper, pacifier, sponge, bottle and bubble pipe. Includes instruction booklet for baby. Circa 1952.

55. AMERICAN CHARACTER 'RICKY JR.' BABY

20". Soft vinyl head, sleep eyes, full rosy cheeks, open mouth, molded brown hair, five-piece soft vinyl baby body. Yellow cotton romper with stitched name, attached glass bottle and wrist booklet. Circa 1954. AMER CHAR DOLL on head.

56. AMERICAN CHARACTER 'RICKY JR.' TODDLER

16". Vinyl head, sleep eyes, open mouth, rooted reddish hair, five-piece vinyl toddler body. Original print romper with white shirt, name sewn on front, ivory snap sandals, attached glass bottle and wrist booklet. Circa 1955. AMER CHAR DOLL on head.

57. AMERICAN CHARACTER 'SANDY McCALL'

35". Vinyl head, sleep eyes with lashes, pug nose with freckles, watermelon smile, five-piece hard plastic child body. Original corduroy jacket and shorts, white cotton shirt, red bolo tie, black and white saddle shoes. Circa 1960. Marked McCALL CORP 1959 on head. Hard-to-find character is in excellent original condition.

58. IDEAL PETITE PATTI PLAYPAL

19". Vinyl head, sleep eyes, closed mouth, rosy cheeks, rooted brown hair, five-piece hard vinyl child body. Original pink cotton dress with dotted pinafore. Circa 1959. Marked IDEAL TOY CORP G18.

59. FORTUNE TOY 'PAM' WITH TWO OUTFITS

8". Hard plastic head, sleep eyes, closed mouth, blonde wig, five-piece hard plastic child body. Mint in original box wearing #9/22 Majorette outfit, baton and original wrist tag. Circa 1955. Includes two boxed outfits, #6/22 Garden Casuals and #6/26 Red Ensemble dress.

60. MADAME ALEXANDER 'MAGGIE WALKER'

20". Hard plastic head that turns when she walks, sleep eyes, closed mouth, auburn saran hair, five-piece hard plastic child body. Tagged original outfit of yellow plaid shirt, ivory cotton skirt with slip and pants, black accented belt. Pink circle tag with beauty box on wrist, original fashion booklet and box. Circa 1952. Unmarked.

61. MADAME ALEXANDER 'MAGGIE WALKER'

17". Hard plastic head which turns as she walks, sleep eyes, closed mouth, brown saran hair, five-piece hard plastic child body. Tagged original outfit #217 of red taffeta redingote over white sleeveless dress, rhinestone buttons. Original boxed beauty set and fashion academy tag. Circa 1952. Unmarked.

(See photograph on page 21)

62. NANCY ANN STORYBOOK 'HOLLY'

5 1/2". Hard plastic head, blue sleep eyes, brown hair, five-piece hard plastic body. Mint original condition in green dress, red felt hat with feathers. Original box with wrist tag and two booklets. Circa 1952. #127 'Holly' from Garden Series.

63. NANCY ANN STORYBOOK 'TOPSY'

5 1/2". Black hard plastic head, black pupil sleep eyes, black hair, five-piece black hard plastic body. Mint, original condition in red dress. Original box, wrist tag and booklet. Circa 1952. #126 'Topsy' from the Fairytale Series.

64. NANCY ANN STORYBOOK 'STAR LIGHT/STAR BRIGHT'

5 1/2". Hard plastic head, blue sleep eyes, blonde hair, five-piece hard plastic body. Mint, original condition, in blue dress with black tulle overlay, silver piping. Original box, wrist tag and booklet. Circa 1952. #173 from the Nursery Rhyme Series.

65. NANCY ANN STORYBOOK 'THE SNOW QUEEN'

5 1/2". Hard plastic head, blue sleep eyes, brown hair, five-piece hard plastic body. Mint, original condition, white dress with tulle overlay, white felt hat with feather. Original box, wrist tag and booklets. Circa 1952. #172 from the Nursery Rhyme Series.

66. NANCY ANN STORYBOOK 'BIG SISTER GOES VISITING'

5 1/2". Hard plastic head, blue sleep eyes, brown hair, five-piece hard plastic body. Mint, original condition, pink/blue print dress, original box and booklet. Circa 1953. #65 from the Big Sister Series.

67. NANCY ANN 'LITTLE SISTER GOES TO SUNDAY SCHOOL'

4 1/2". Hard plastic head, black pupil sleep eyes, brown hair, four-piece hard plastic body. Mint, original condition, red/multi-polka dot print dress, original box, wrist tag and booklet. Circa 1953. #54 from the Little Sister Series.

68. NANCY ANN 'LITTLE SISTER GOES TO SCHOOL'

4 1/2". Hard plastic head, black pupil sleep eyes, blonde hair, four-piece hard plastic body. Mint, original condition, blue/floral print dress, original box, wrist tag and booklet. Circa 1953. #50 from the Little Sister Series.

69. MADAME ALEXANDER 'QUEEN ELIZABETH II'

18". Hard plastic Margaret head which turns when she walks, blue sleep eyes, closed mouth, amber curled and upswept hair, five-piece hard plastic child body. Tagged original ivory brocade gown with hoop slip, blue Order of the Garter sash with rhinestone/pearl accents and white mitts. Rhinestone jewelry includes three bracelets, earrings and tiara. Original box is included. Circa 1954. Unmarked. Exceptional coloring adds to her originality.

70. MADAME ALEXANDER 'PRINCE CHARLES' ALEXANDER-KIN

7 1/2". Hard plastic head that turns when walking, grey sleep eyes, closed mouth, blonde hair, seven-piece hard plastic child body. Original navy-blue jacket, shorts and cap, white shirt. Circa 1957. Marked ALEX on back. Catalogue #397.

71. MADAME ALEXANDER 'PRINCESS ANNE' ALEXANDER-KIN

7 1/2". Hard plastic head that turns when she walks, grey sleep eyes, closed mouth, blonde hair, seven-piece hard plastic child body. Original tagged white lace dress with pink petticoat, white straw bonnet with pink ribbon. Original box with original tan side-snap shoes. Circa 1957. Marked ALEX on back. Catalogue #396.

72. MADAME ALEXANDER WENDYKINS

7 1/2". Hard plastic head turns when she walks, grey sleep eyes, closed mouth, blonde hair, five-piece hard plastic child body. Tagged pink organdy dress with lace accents, cotton slip/panties, straw hat with flowers. Circa 1954. Marked ALEX on back. Early straight-leg walker.

73. MADAME ALEXANDER WENDYKINS

7 1/2". Hard plastic head turns when walking, grey sleep eyes, closed mouth, brown hair, five-piece hard plastic child body. Tagged pink swiss-dot dress with matching panties. Circa 1955. Marked ALEX on back.

74. MADAME ALEXANDER WENDYKINS

7 1/2". Hard plastic head turns when she walks, black sleep eyes, closed mouth, brown hair, seven-piece hard plastic child body. Tagged white organdy dress with red rick-rack trim, red panties, red straw hat. Circa 1957. Marked ALEX on back.

75. MADAME ALEXANDER WENDYKINS

7 1/2". Hard plastic head turns when she walks, grey sleep eyes, closed mouth, auburn hair, seven-piece hard plastic child body. Turquoise and white striped dress with matching panties, original box. Circa 1957. Marked ALEX on back.

76. EFFANBEE TINTAIR HONEY DOLL

16". Hard plastic head, blue sleep eyes, closed mouth, platinum hair, five-piece hard plastic child body. White organdy dress with pastel flowers, pink shoes with bows. Includes wrist tag with curlers, tintair coloring kit with 'Glossy Chestnut' and 'Carrot Top' colors, plastic cape to protect doll, original box. Circa 1951. Pristine, original condition with vivid coloring.

77. IDEAL TONI DOLL

19". Hard plastic head, grey sleep eyes, closed mouth, brown hair, five-piece hard plastic child body. Original multi-color plaid rayon jumper/blouse combination dress. Circa 1952. Marked Ideal Doll on head/P-19 on back. Faint leg marks.

78. IDEAL TONI DOLL

16". Hard plastic head, grey sleep eyes, closed mouth, blonde hair, five-piece hard plastic child body. Red and white organdy dress with rick-rack trim. Circa 1952. Marked P-91 Ideal Doll Made in USA on head/P-91 on back.

79. IDEAL TONI DOLL WITH BOX

16". Hard plastic head, blue sleep eyes, closed mouth, black nylon hair, five-piece hard plastic child body. Tagged multi-color plaid jumper with blouse, original wrist tag, box and Toni Play Wave solution set. Beautiful matte facial finish. Circa 1952. Marked P-90 Ideal Doll Made in USA on head/P-90 on back.

80. MADAME ALEXANDER CINDERELLA GIFT SET

14". Hard plastic Margaret head, blue sleep eyes, closed mouth, blonde wig, five-piece hard plastic child body. Original store display centers Poor Cinderella in tattered dress, apron and scarf holding a broom. Around her is a white and silver ballgown, gold snood, gold braid and rhinestone tiara, silver magic wand, "glass" slippers and wedding pieces including net veil, bouquet, stockings and lingerie trousseau. Displayed against original peach cardboard background. Original clover wrist tag. Circa 1952. Marked ALEX faintly on head. (An exceptional and rare set never before documented.)

81. MADAME ALEXANDER ALICE IN WONDERLAND

20". Hard plastic Maggie face, blue sleep eyes, closed mouth, blonde hair, five-piece hard plastic child body. Original tagged blue taffeta dress (now faded to lilac and soiled to one side) with white organdy pinafore, white cotton slip with attached bloomers with blue bows. Original wrist booklet and beauty set attached to wrist. Circa 1951. Unmarked.

82. MADAME ALEXANDER RARE KATHRYN GRAYSON PORTRAIT

on cover of this book

21". Hard plastic head, grey sleep eyes with lush eyelashes and brown eyeliner, closed full mouth, hand-painted arched brows, strawberry-brown hair, polished fingernails, five-piece hard plastic child body. Original peach satin gown with tulle skirt and bodice overlaid with lace and rhinestones. Accessories include pearl-drop earrings, rhinestone bracelet and floral hairsprays. Circa 1949. Marked ALEX faintly on head. (Inspired by the movie "Midnight Kiss", this extremely rare portrait, in pristine condition, is sensuous as well as graceful.)

on Cover!

83. EFFANBEE HONEY WALKER

18". Hard plastic head that turns when walking, blue sleep eyes, closed mouth, honey-blonde hair in pigtails, five-piece hard plastic child body. Original blue and white cotton dress (with original price tag attached), black belt. Includes wrist tag with curlers, instruction sheet, and blue box. Circa 1952. Marked EFFANBEE on head and back.

84. EFFANBEE HONEY WALKER

18". Hard plastic head which turns when walking, blue sleep eyes, closed mouth, brown hair curled under, five-piece hard plastic child body. Lilac taffeta dress with ruffled bodice, nylon slip and panties. Circa 1954. Marked EFFANBEE on head.

85. IDEAL HARRIET HUBBARD AYER BEAUTY DOLL

15". Soft vinyl head, sleep eyes, closed mouth, blonde hair, five-piece vinyl child body. Original grey waffle-weave cotton dress with red striped pinafore. Original wrist tags and make-up table with cosmetics to apply to the doll, box with instructions. Circa 1953. Marked Ideal Doll MK-15 on head, Ideal Doll P-91 on back.

86. CONSTANCE BANNISTER'S BANNISTER BABY BY HORSMAN

17". Soft vinyl head, sleep eyes, open mouth, molded hair, five-piece vinyl baby body. Original pink plush hooded cover with extra dress, socks, bottle and bubble pipe. Vividly packaged with box doubling as a carry case. Produced by the Sun Rubber Company of Ohio. Circa 1957. Marked Constance Bannister New York on head.

87. IDEAL SARALEE BABY

18". Soft brown vinyl head, sleep eyes, closed mouth, molded hair, vinyl limbs attached to brown cloth body with working Mama crier. Original white organdy dress and bonnet with yellow accents, wrist tag attached. Circa 1955. Marked Ideal Doll C-17 on head.

88. BELLE CHARACTER BABY

17". Soft vinyl head, sleep eyes, closed mouth, rosy cheeks, molded hair, one-piece rubber body. Original nylon christening gown and bonnet, pink and blue box. Circa 1955. Unmarked. Wonderful molded character expression to face.

89. MADAME ALEXANDER PEGGY BRIDE

17". Hard plastic Margaret head, blue sleep eyes, closed mouth, blonde curled hair, five-piece hard plastic child body. Original (frail) tagged bridal gown, bouquet, headpiece with veil, stockings, blue ribbon garter, panties. Clover wrist tag attached. Circa 1950. Marked ALEXANDER on head. Wonderfully fresh body tone and facial coloring.

90. MADAME ALEXANDER RINGBEARER

12". Hard plastic head, blue sleep eyes, closed mouth, thick blonde hair, five-piece hard plastic toddler body. Original ivory satin one-piece suit with lace accents, muslin boxers, carries satin pillow with rhinestone ring in center. Circa 1950. Marked ALEXANDER on head. Hard-to-find character is Lovey-Dovey from the 1948 catalogue. The wig is applied over his molded hair.

91. MADAME ALEXANDER BRIDEGROOM

18". Hard plastic head, blue sleep eyes with shadow, closed mouth, reddish caracul wig, five-piece hard plastic child body. Detailed original outfit of black tuxedo with tails, satin lapels, boutonniere, white shirt with attached cummerbund, bow tie, watch fob and felt top hat. Complete with labeled original box. Circa 1950. Marked ALEXANDER on head.

92. VOGUE GINNY WALKER WITH ORIGINAL BOX
7 1/2". Hard plastic head that turns when walking, brown sleep eyes, brown hair, five-piece hard plastic child body. Undressed doll with pink panties, socks and shoes in original pink and white labeled box with Ginny Club News and instruction sheet. Also includes extra Ginny vinyl parasol and pillowcase. Circa 1954. Marked Ginny Vogue Dolls Inc. Pat Pend Made in USA.

93. VOGUE GINNY WITH ORIGINAL BOX
7 1/2". Hard plastic head, blue sleep eyes, bright red hair with original rubberband, five-piece hard plastic child body. Original blue organdy eyelet dress with lace and floral accents, blue straw bonnet with flowers, blue socks and front snap shoes. Pink original box with advertisement page labeled "Vogue Dolls, Inc. Fashion Leaders in Doll Society". Circa 1952. Marked Vogue Doll on back. Doll is #61 'Cathy' from the Debutante Series.

94. BOXED GINNY OUTFIT
#186 My Flowered Robe, circa 1955.

95. BOXED GINNY OUTFIT
#7145 Ballerina includes silver tutu with blue tulle, floral garland, satin ballet slippers, brochure. Circa 1957.

96. BOXED GINNY OUTFIT
#6185 Yellow felt coat with black headband, yellow purse. Circa 1956.

97. BOXED GINNY'S PUP
#6831 Steiff mohair terrier with ear button and tag, plain vinyl blanket with name, leash, bell with bow. Circa 1956.

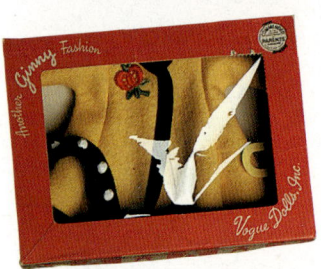

98. VOGUE GINNY BRIDEGROOM
7". Hard plastic head, unusual turquoise and hazel eyes, blonde hair, five-piece hard plastic child body. Tagged original black felt tailcoat and top hat, white plastic vest with collar, grey felt pants, Vogue Doll wrist tag. Circa 1952. Marked Vogue Doll on back.

99. VOGUE GINNY BRIDE
7 1/2". Hard plastic head, bright blue sleep eyes, brown hair, five-piece hard plastic child body. Original white satin gown with attached trailing flowers, gold and lace edging, Juliet-type cap with veil, satin panties with blue trim, blue ribbon garter, open plastic Bible and wrist tag. Circa 1952. Marked Vogue Doll on back.

100. BOXED GINNY OUTFIT
#6123 Kinder Crowd outfit, green/white pattern dress and panties, Ginny headband, socks and green shoes. Circa 1956.

101. TWO BOXED GINNY OUTFITS
#675 Whiz Kids yellow vinyl raincoat, pouch with black boots, black molded sou'wester hat. Circa 1954. #130 yellow knit skirt and cap with "Ginny" top, yellow socks, black shoes, brown eye glasses included.

102. BOXED GINNY OUTFIT
#121 Kinder Crowd purple checked dress with vinyl whales and belt, matching panties, hairbow, socks, shoes. Circa 1955.

103. BOXED GINNY OUTFIT
#6138 Merry Moppets grey and pink organdy dress and bloomers, socks, shoes and pink straw bonnet. Circa 1956.

104. BOXED GINNY OUTFIT
#7143 Plaid shirt, grey kiltie skirt, matching shorts, red felt hat, socks, shoes, red purse, white plastic gloves. Circa 1957.

105. BOXED GINNY OUTFIT
#1304 Shirtdress with white top, plaid skirt, nylon panties and white plastic belt, brochure. Circa 1958.

106. BOXED GINNY OUTFIT
#242 Tiny Miss white organdy dress with blue ribbon, panties, cap with flower, socks and shoes. Circa 1955.

107. BOXED GINNY OUTFIT
#352 And Away We Go red cotton dress, panties, green knit tennis-motif top, white belt, socks, green shoes, green bead bracelet and necklace, green felt hat. Circa 1955.

108. MADAME ALEXANDER 'BABS' THE ICE SKATER

14". Hard plastic Margaret head, blue sleep eyes, closed mouth, rosy cheeks, unusual-styled blonde wig, five-piece hard plastic child body. Original tagged white satin skating costume with marabou trim and gold braiding, matching panties, floral and gilt headpiece, original box. Circa 1949. Beautifully preserved, fresh skin-tone coloring.

109. AMERICAN CHARACTER 'TONI'

20". Vinyl head, blue sleep eyes, closed mouth, auburn rooted hair in bouffant style, seven-piece hard vinyl adult modelled body (jointed ankles). Ivory satin and taffeta gown with puffed sleeves, gathered and graduated color overskirt accented with rhinestones at the waist, hoop skirt petticoat, hose, rhinestone necklace and floral hairsprays. Circa 1958. Unmarked.

110. AMERICAN CHARACTER 'TONI' WITH BOX

19". Vinyl head, blue sleep eyes with shadow, closed mouth, rooted blonde hair, five-piece adult modelled body. Original blue taffeta dress with gathered hem, gem brooch, black bag, pearl ring, necklace and earrings, taffeta cloche. Pink and blue box with #206 on the label. Circa 1958. Marked AMERICAN CHAR in circle on lower back. This doll was also named 'Sweet Sue Sophisticate'.

111. VALENTINE 'AIDA' BALLERINA

18". Vinyl head turns when her legs dance, blue sleep eyes, closed mouth, rooted blonde hair, five-piece hard plastic body with muscular legs, toes on pointe. Original Nutcracker tutu of fuchsia tulle with matching panties, vinyl ballet toe shoes by Capezio in original box with brochure. Circa 1958. Marked 59 VW on head. Legs are ingeniously designed to fully arc for positioning.

112. EEGEE "LIL' SUSAN" BALLERINA

11". Vinyl head that turns when dancing, blue sleep eyes, closed mouth, brown hair, seven-piece hard plastic toddler body. Original red metallic tutu with silver glitter accents, ballet shoes, brochure in original box. Circa 1958. Marked EEGEE on head. Style #23/03X.

113. NANCY ANN 'GAIETY' STYLE SHOW DOLL

18". Hard plastic head that turns when walked, grey sleep eyes with shadow, closed red mouth, blonde hair, five-piece hard plastic child body. Original nylon dress with aqua striping, rose ribbon and black lace accents, hoop underskirt, hose, and black strap shoes. On her head she wears an ostrich plume with rhinestone accent, carries a black hatbox and is covered by a black lace shawl. Circa 1950. Unmarked. A stunning example of costuming by the Nancy Ann designers.

(See photograph on page 37)

114. NANCY ANN 'LAWN PARTY' STYLE SHOW DOLL

18". Hard plastic head, grey sleep eyes with shadow, closed mouth, brown hair, five-piece hard plastic child body. Original long cotton pink dress with rosebud pattern and lace accents, black velvet bow, hoop underskirt, black snap shoes, large straw sunbonnet with flowers. Circa 1950. Unmarked.

115. NANCY ANN 'DINNER DATE' STYLE SHOW DOLL

18". Hard plastic head, grey sleep eyes with shadow, closed mouth, rosy cheeks, brown hair, five-piece hard plastic child body. Original peach taffeta gown with black lace overlay, peach ribbon and corsage, hoop underskirt, hose, gold snap shoes, original silver wrist tag. Circa 1950. Unmarked. Original box with Grand Bal label.

116. NANCY ANN 'WHITE LILACS' STYLE SHOW DOLL

18". Hard plastic head, grey sleep eyes with shadow, closed mouth, brown hair, five-piece hard plastic child body. Original long white cotton dress with aqua rosebuds and bodice, cotton hoop underskirt, hose, lace up flats, straw bonnet with flowers. Circa 1953. Unmarked.

117. MADAME ALEXANDER 'ANNABELLE'

14". Hard plastic Maggie head, blue sleep eyes, closed mouth, blonde hair with bow, five-piece hard plastic child body. Original tagged outfit of white cotton dress with red rick-rack trim, red knit pullover with stitched name, cotton petticoat and panty, beauty set attached to wrist. Original labeled box. Circa 1952. Unmarked. Kate Smith's Annabelle, style #1510.

118. AMERICAN CHARACTER 'SWEET SUE' WALKER

20". Hard plastic head that turns when walked, blue sleep eyes, closed mouth, blonde wig, five-piece hard plastic child body. Red and white embossed, cotton chintz dress with red front-snap shoes, straw hat. Circa 1955. Unmarked.

Close-up of exceptional hair floral spray.

119. MADAME ALEXANDER 'MARGOT' BALLERINA

14". Hard plastic Maggie face, blue sleep eyes, closed mouth, light-brown hair in black net snood, five-piece hard plastic child body. Tagged original blue satin and organdy tutu with floral and gold loop accenting, matching panty, black velvet choker, ballet flats and clover wrist tag attached. Circa 1953. Unmarked.

120. MADAME ALEXANDER FASHION LADY

14". Hard plastic Margaret head, blue sleep eyes, closed mouth, flame hair, five-piece hard plastic child body. Tagged original mauve taffeta gown with pink satin inset at hip, pink full slip, panty and hose. Accessories include floral hair spray to side of head, "crystal" necklace and ostrich plume fan. Circa 1954. Original clover wrist tag. From the "Fashions of a Century" series, a rare doll, undocumented prior to this edition.

121. MADAME ALEXANDER 'WENDY ANN'

7 1/2". Hard plastic head, grey sleep eyes, closed red mouth, auburn wig, five-piece hard plastic child body. White organdy dress with embroidered cherries at hem, matching panty, green straw bonnet with flowers, Alexander-kins box. Circa 1953. Marked ALEX on back.

122. MADAME ALEXANDER 'WENDY ANN'

7 1/2". Hard plastic head, grey sleep eyes, rosy blush, closed red mouth, blonde wig, five-piece hard plastic child body. Tagged light blue organdy "storybook" dress with lace ruffles and accents over pink taffeta petticoat and pantaloons, plastic water can with garden tools. Original Wendy-Ann wrist tag and box marked #552. Circa 1953. Marked ALEX on back.

123. MADAME ALEXANDER 'WENDY-ANN'

7 1/2". Hard plastic head, grey sleep eyes, closed red mouth, blonde wig, five-piece hard plastic child body. Tagged pink or red gingham dress with organdy inset and sleeves, matching panty, large straw bonnet with ribbon, original box marked 534. Circa 1953. Marked ALEX on back.

124. MADAME ALEXANDER 'MAGGIE MIX-UP'

7 1/2". Hard plastic head that turns when walking, green sleep eyes, watermelon smile, red wig, bent knee, hard plastic child body. Pink gingham shirt with denim overall, pink conical sunhat, plastic water can, original wrist tag. Circa 1961. Marked ALEX on back.

125. MADAME ALEXANDER 'SOUTHERN BELLE'

8". Hard plastic head, grey sleep eyes, closed mouth, blonde wig, bent-knee walker, hard plastic child body. Tagged blue taffeta dress with lace ruffles and accents, petticoat, pantaloons, matching bonnet with flowers, wrist booklet. Circa 1964. Marked ALEX on back. *Little Women booklet*

126. MADAME ALEXANDER BRIDE

8". Hard plastic head, grey sleep eyes, closed mouth, blonde wig, bent knee, hard plastic child body. Tagged white net wedding gown with attached organdy slip (#735), floral veil headpiece, bouquet, pink garter with rhinestone. Circa 1966. Marked ALEX on back.

127. MADAME ALEXANDER WENDY-KINS

7 1/2". Hard plastic head, grey sleep eyes, closed mouth, blonde wig, bent knee walker, hard plastic child body. Tagged chambray coat with red lining, matching hat. Circa 1956. Marked ALEX on back.

128. MADAME ALEXANDER 'McGUFFEY ANA'

8". Hard plastic head, grey sleep eyes, closed mouth, blonde braided wig, bent knee, hard plastic child body. Tagged red gingham dress with white eyelet pinafore, cotton petticoat, pantaloons, cotton hose, floral straw bonnet, original box. Circa 1965. Marked ALEX on back.

129. MADAME ALEXANDER 'CISSETTE'

10". Hard plastic head, grey sleep eyes, closed mouth, brown wig, bent knee, hard plastic, adult body. Tagged pink nylon slip and panty with lace edging, gold strap heels, pearl earrings, original box. Circa 1957-63. Marked MME ALEXANDER on back. Beautiful facial color.

130. MADAME ALEXANDER 'CISSETTE'

10". Hard plastic head, grey sleep eyes, closed mouth, auburn wig, bent knee, hard plastic, adult body. Tagged navy taffeta dress with white organdy shoulder wrap, white taffeta slip and panty, hose, black strap heels, pearl bracelet and white floral straw bonnet. Original box and brochure. Circa 1957-63. Marked MME ALEXANDER on back.

131. MADAME ALEXANDER 'CISSETTE' AS NUN

10". Hard plastic head, grey sleep eyes, closed mouth, brown wig, bent knee, hard plastic adult body. Unmarked, tailored white cotton habit with wimple, pearl bead rosary. Circa 1957-63. Marked MME ALEXANDER on back.

132. MADAME ALEXANDER 'CISSETTE' AS NUN

10". Hard plastic head, grey sleep eyes, closed mouth, cropped blonde wig, bent knee, hard plastic adult body. Unmarked, tailored black habit with wimple, black bead rosary. Circa 1957-63. Marked MME ALEXANDER on back.

133. MADAME ALEXANDER 'CISSY'

20". Hard plastic head, blue sleep eyes, closed mouth, blonde wig, bent knee, hard plastic adult body, vinyl arms. Tagged, navy taffeta fashion dress with tulle cap sleeves, petticoat, white fur stole, blue net and feather headpiece, pearl bracelet, necklace and earrings, hose, black open heels. Circa 1958. Marked ALEXANDER on head.

134. MADAME ALEXANDER 'CISSY'

20". Hard plastic head, blue sleep eyes, closed mouth, blonde wig, bent knee, hard plastic adult body, vinyl arms. Tagged organdy polka-dot dress with red sash, red straw hat with veil, petticoat, hose, red open heels, hatbox. Circa 1958. Marked ALEXANDER on head.

135. MADAME ALEXANDER 'GODEY GROOM'

14". Hard plastic Maggie head, blue sleep eyes, closed mouth, blonde cut and styled wig, five-piece hard plastic child body. Tagged original black tuxedo jacket with tails, white satin shirt with rhinestone accent, boutonniere, white bow tie, fob, brown pants with satin piping. Circa 1949. Unmarked.

136. MADAME ALEXANDER 'GODEY BRIDE'

14". Hard plastic Margaret head, blue sleep eyes, closed mouth, blonde elaborately-coiffed wig, five-piece hard plastic child body. Tagged original white satin gown with fitted waist-piece and bustle back, shaped lace and net veil, bouquet, pantaloons, hose, clover wrist tag. Circa 1949. Unmarked.

Close-up view of exceptional hair design.

137. MADAME ALEXANDER 'ELISE' BALLERINA

15". Vinyl head, blue sleep eyes, closed mouth, blonde wig, hard plastic, adult bent-knee body with jointed ankles, jointed vinyl arms. Tagged blue satin and tulle tutu with floral accent, pink stockings, ballet shoes, floral headpiece, rhinestone earrings, original box. Circa 1964. Marked ALEXANDER C 1964 on head, MME ALEXANDER on back. Elise ballerina style #1715.

138. EFFANBEE 'MELODIE - THE SINGING DOLL WITH THE GOLDEN VOICE'

28". Vinyl head, blue sleep eyes, closed mouth, curly auburn rooted hair, seven-piece hard plastic child body, bendable knees. Original organdy and nylon dress with floral pattern, straw bonnet, satin sash, wrist booklet. Circa 1953-1956. Unmarked. Back plate removes for battery insertion and also houses record player.

138A. IDEAL 'SAUCY WALKER' WITH ORIGINAL BOX

22". Hard plastic head, flirty blue sleep eyes, open mouth, auburn hair in ponytail, five-piece hard plastic toddler body with working crier. Original blue cotton waffle weave dress with printed pinafore and panty, wrist booklet and box. Circa 1952. Marked IDEAL DOLL on head and back.

139. IDEAL 'PRINCESS MARY'

19". Vinyl head, green sleep eyes, closed mouth, brown rooted hair, five-piece hard plastic child body. Original multi-colored striped rayon dress with floral accent, gold front snap shoes. Original wrist tag, Ideal tag with curlers, labelled box. Circa 1955. Marked V92 Ideal Doll on head, Ideal Doll 19 on back.

140. SAYCO DREAM GIRL

20". Vinyl head, green sleep eyes, closed mouth, brown rooted hair, five-piece hard vinyl adult body. Original cotton gown brushed with gold accented with gold lace, nylon panty, hose, gold open-toe heel, pearl-drop earrings. Original box and wrist tag. Circa 1955-57. Marked 10 on head.

141. IDEAL 'BONNIE BRAIDS' TODDLER

14". Vinyl head which turns when walking, blue sleep eyes, open mouth with three painted teeth, molded yellow hair with two tufts of saran hair extending from top, five-piece hard plastic toddler body. Original calico print dress, wrist tag and toothbrush tied with ribbon. Circa 1952. Marked Copyright 1951 Chicago Tribune Ideal Doll on head.

142. IDEAL POSIE TODDLER

17". Vinyl head, blue sleep eyes, closed mouth, blonde rooted hair, five-piece hard plastic toddler body, grill in stomach. Original printed cotton blend dress with ribbon and trim, Saucy Walker wrist tag and brown box. Circa 1955. Marked Ideal Doll VP 17 on head, Ideal Doll 16 on body.

143. IDEAL LAYETTE FOR 'HONEYSUCKLE' DOLL

Mini layette set in original packaging for Ideal baby doll includes gown and bonnet, booties, blanket, knit top, soap, sponge and small tin of talc with original tag. Whimsical box design with Ideal logo intertwined with assorted baby dolls. Circa 1950.

144. IDEAL SHIRLEY TEMPLE

12". Vinyl head, hazel sleep eyes, open mouth with teeth, rooted blonde curls, five-piece hard vinyl child body. Original tagged pink lingerie set, black front snap shoes, socks, wrist booklet and white with gold star labelled box. Circa 1958. Marked Ideal Doll ST-12 on head, Ideal Doll St-12-N on back.

145. IDEAL SHIRLEY TEMPLE

12". Vinyl head, hazel sleep eyes, open mouth with teeth, rooted blonde curls, five-piece hard vinyl child body. Original blue nylon dress with floral and lace accents, black v-front shoes, socks, pink straw bonnet, original black, orange and white box. Includes additional blue and white romper with name pin. Circa 1957-59. Marked Ideal Doll ST-12 head, Ideal Doll ST-12-N back.

146. IDEAL SHIRLEY TEMPLE

12". Vinyl head, hazel sleep eyes, open mouth with teeth, rooted blonde curls, five-piece hard vinyl child body. Original tagged pink and blue nylon party dress, slip, panty, name pin, black v- front shoes, socks, wrist tag, black and orange box. Circa 1957- 59. Marked Ideal Doll ST-12 on head, Ideal Doll ST-12-N on back.

147. IDEAL SHIRLEY TEMPLE

12". Vinyl head, hazel sleep eyes, open mouth with teeth, rooted blonde curls, five-piece hard vinyl child body. Original tagged "Wee Willie Winkie" Scottish outfit, pink slip and panty, name pin, black v-front shoes, socks. Circa 1958. Marked Ideal Doll ST-12 on head, Ideal Doll ST-12-N on back.

148. IDEAL SHIRLEY TEMPLE

12". Vinyl head, hazel sleep eyes, open mouth with teeth, rooted blonde curls, five-piece hard vinyl child body. Original outdoors outfit includes vinyl jacket with plush collar, felt pants and cap, orange scarf, black v-front shoes. Includes additional orange and white print dress with name pin, cotton panty, orange and black box. Circa 1957-59. Marked Ideal Doll ST-12 on head, Ideal Doll ST-12-N on back.

149. IDEAL SHIRLEY TEMPLE

12". Vinyl head, hazel sleep eyes, open mouth with teeth, rooted blonde curls, five-piece hard vinyl child body. Original Pollyana outfit of plaid shirt, blue pants with plaid cuff, straw hat, red purse, black v-front shoes, original black and orange box. Circa 1957-59. Marked Ideal Doll ST-12 on head, Ideal Doll ST-12-N back.

150. IDEAL SHIRLEY TEMPLE GIFT SET

12". Vinyl head, hazel sleep eyes, open mouth with teeth, rooted blonde curls, five-piece hard vinyl body. Set includes assorted clothing including blue dress with rick-rack trim, pink slip, aqua nylon dress, teal and white print dress, white hat, red vinyl raincoat, hat and bag. Doll is wearing red and white skirt with red quilt-type jacket, red straw hat, black v-front shoes, socks, red name purse. Original name pin, pearl necklace, blue glasses, wrist tag. Case resembles a television set with clear "screen" front, pictures on all sides. Circa 1958. Mint condition.

151. IDEAL SHIRLEY TEMPLE IN BOX

15". Vinyl head, hazel sleep eyes, open mouth with teeth, rooted blonde curls, five-piece hard vinyl body. Original tagged yellow nylon dress with lace trim, blue floral appliques and name pin, cotton panty, white side-button shoes, socks, white purse, wrist tag, box marked #1400. Circa 1958. Marked Ideal Doll ST-15-N.

151A. ASSORTED SHIRLEY TEMPLE FASHIONS

Includes pink slip, yellow nylon party dress with ribbons, navy taffeta dress with red print jacket, red purse, red straw bonnet, black v-front shoes with socks in plastic pouch. Original box.

151B. ASSORTED SHIRLEY TEMPLE FASHIONS

Includes Pollyana-type set still stapled into box, red purse, black v-front shoes in plastic, two pairs white socks, red and white pajama set, yellow fluffy coat, nylon slip, yellow cotton one-piece with yellow and white striped skirt. Original box.

152. EMMETT KELLY'S WILLIE THE CLOWN

15". Vinyl head, painted facial features, hair and hat, one-piece latex body. Original tagged cotton and felt clown outfit, colorful box. Circa 1955. Marked BB on head for Baby Barry Toy Co of New York.

153. EMMETT KELLY'S WILLIE THE CLOWN

15". Vinyl head, painted facial features, hair and hat, one-piece latex body. Original tagged cotton and felt clown outfit, colorful box. Circa 1955. Marked BB on head for Baby Barry Toy Co. Note the different colored outfit and facial distinctions from the above.

154. HORSMAN CAMPBELL KID

12". Vinyl head, painted facial features, molded hair, three-piece soft vinyl toddler body. Original blue cotton playsuit with white apron and chef's hat, original tag, price tag and box. Circa 1953. Unmarked.

155. NANCY ANN 'MUFFIE' WALKER
7". Hard plastic head that turns when walking, blue sleep eyes, closed mouth, brown braided wig, five-piece hard plastic child body. Circa 1955. Marked Storybook Dolls California MUFFIE on back.

156. NANCY ANN 'MUFFIE' WALKER
7". Hard plastic head that turns when walking, brown sleep eyes, closed mouth, blonde braided wig, five-piece hard plastic child body. Original tagged red and blue polka-dot dress, red shoes. Original pink polka-dot box. Circa 1955. Marked Storybook Dolls California MUFFIE on back.

157. DELUXE 'SWEET AMY' DRESS-ME DOLL
17". Vinyl head, blue sleep eyes, closed mouth, rooted blonde hair, one-piece latex body. Original cotton print dress with pajamas and raincoat, beauty set, original tag and box. Circa 1954. Marked 3 in circle on head.

158. ARRANBEE 'LITTLEST ANGEL' WALKER IN BOX
10 1/2". Hard plastic head, blue sleep eyes, closed mouth, blonde wig, seven-piece (jointed knees) hard plastic toddler body. Original white nylon dress with red hearts, white bonnet, red vinyl strap shoes. Circa 1955. Marked R & B on head.

159. 'ROBERTA ANN' BRIDE DOLL

18". Hard plastic head, green sleep eyes with shadow, closed mouth, brown saran wig, five-piece hard plastic child body. Original ivory satin and tulle gown, headpiece with veil, bouquet, wrist tag and original box. Circa 1952. Unmarked.

160. TWO DOLL FASHIONS BY DANDEE

Two mint-in-box dresses for 11 1/2" dolls by Dandee of Philadelphia, Pa. Pink strapless satin and net dress with silver bag and pink dotted nylon dress with white collar.

161. ROBERTA'S GLAMOUR DOLL

19". Vinyl head, blue sleep eyes, closed mouth, rooted auburn wig, five-piece hard plastic and vinyl adult body. Original blue nylon and tulle gown with flowers, pearl earrings, floral headpiece, original box. Circa 1957. Marked AE 2006-1 on head.

162. UNEEDA 'TINYTEEN' IN BOX

10". Vinyl head, blue sleep eyes, closed mouth, rooted reddish hair, six-piece (turning waist) hard vinyl, adult body. Original strapless white and gold nylon gown, white hat, pearl earrings, wrist tag and box marked #1206 "Beautime". Circa 1957-60. Marked UNEEDA on head.

163. UNEEDA 'TINYTEEN' BRIDE IN BOX

10". Vinyl head, blue sleep eyes, closed mouth, rooted blonde hair, six-piece (turning waist) hard vinyl, adult body. Original white nylon and net gown with veil, bouquet, pearl earrings, wrist tag and box marked #1201 "Bridetime". Circa 1957-60. Marked P in circle on head.

164. MYSTERY DOLL ATTRIBUTED TO ROBERTA

14". Hard plastic head, blue sleep eyes, open mouth with four teeth, felt tongue, auburn wig, five-piece hard plastic child body. Nude, but with three packaged accessories by SB Novelty Co, including gold nylon snood, nylon panty and garters. Circa 1956. Marked 14 on head, made in USA in circle on back. Original pink box.

165. '14R' FASHION DOLL

19". Vinyl head, blue sleep eyes with purple shadow, closed red mouth, rosy cheeks, rooted blonde hair, seven-piece (swivel waist) hard plastic, adult body. Original navy taffeta dress with full slip, matching jacket, pink scarf and hat, navy open-toe heels with flowers, rhinestone earrings and ring (has caused greening to finger), generic fashion doll box with #2006. Circa 1957-1959. Marked 14R on head. A number of companies used the 14R mark on the dolls during this time period. Although all have similar characteristics, it is hard to attribute them to one firm. They vary in quality of doll and costume. Some were given as carnival prizes.

166. AMERICAN CHARACTER 'BETSY McCALL'

14". Vinyl head, blue sleep eyes, watermelon smile, light-brown rooted hair, seven-piece (swivel waist) hard plastic child body. Original plaid skirt with attached top, separate sailor-type top overneath, blue and red hat. Circa 1958. Marked McCall Corp 1958, in circle.

167. AMERICAN CHARACTER 'TONI'

10". Vinyl head, grey sleep eyes, closed mouth, rooted light-brown hair, five-piece adult hard plastic body. Beige coat, straw hat and hose. Circa 1958. Marked American Character in circle on back.

168. RICHWOOD TOYS 'SANDRA SUE' TWIN SET

Pair of 8" dolls with hard plastic heads, blue sleep eyes, closed mouths, blonde and auburn hair, delicate five-piece hard plastic bodies. One wears original purple plaid dress with yellow organdy pinafore (F-68), the other in slip. Duplicate outfit is included with original store polybag and original pamphlet. Circa 1956. Auburn marked 3 and 1 inside arms, blonde marked 2 only.

169. WOODEN SANDRA SUE SWING SET

Red wooden swing, with side support poles and "grass"-covered base. Has never been assembled and comes complete in original brown box with "Sandra Sue Swing" on side.

170. VOGUE 'GINNETTE' IN BOX

8". Vinyl head, blue sleep eyes, open mouth, molded hair, five-piece vinyl baby body. Blue and white crocheted dress and bonnet with white nylon slip and diapers. Includes original pink corduroy

romper with pink knit top, labeled glass bottle, pair of pink shoes and socks in original vogue package, two brochures. Circa 1956. Unmarked.

171. GINNETTE THREE-PIECE NURSERY SET

Three pieces of wooden nursery furniture includes baby tender, bath/bassinet combination and drop-side crib with mattress and pillow. All are sturdy wooden pieces of high quality, painted white then stenciled with animals and "Ginnette" name.

172. GINNY WOODEN BED

Pink wooden youth bed with half-side rails and "Ginny" name stenciled at end. Original well-labelled box.

173. ASSORTED GINNETTE CLOTHING

Includes polka-dot flannel diapers and robe, assorted panties, floral nylon bed jacket and hat, two cotton bed jackets and pink wool herringbone coat and hat, plastic bottle and rattle.

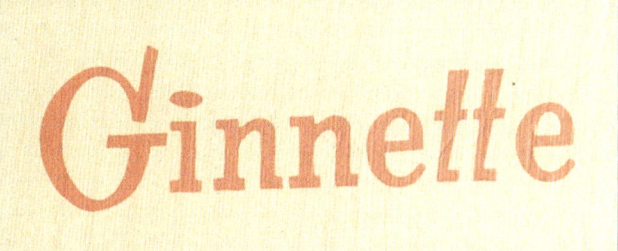

174. VIRGA 'TINY TWINKLE' BALLERINA

8". *Hard plastic head that turns when walked, blue sleep eyes, closed mouth, brunette wig, five-piece hard plastic child body with pointed feet. Original pink color-splashed tutu with aqua tulle, pink rubber toe shoes. Circa 1957. Unmarked. Original unfolding box can be made into a stage for the doll.*

175. VIRGA 'TINY TWINKLE' BALLERINA

8". *Hard plastic head that turns when walked, blue sleep eyes, closed mouth, light-brown hair, five-piece hard plastic child body with pointed feet. Original pink splash tutu with pink tulle, pink rubber toe shoes. Circa 1957. Unmarked. Original "stage" box.*

176. VIRGA 'TINY TWINKLE' BALLERINA

8". *Hard plastic head that turns when walked, blue sleep eyes, closed mouth, brown wig, five-piece hard plastic child body with pointed feet. Original pink splash tutu with blue tulle, pink toe shoes. Circa 1957. Unmarked. Original "stage" presentation box.*

177. VIRGA 'PLAY-MATES' BRIDE

8". *Hard plastic head that turns when walked, blue sleep eyes, closed mouth, light-brown wig, five-piece hard plastic child body. Original white nylon gown, net veil, bouquet and shoes. Circa 1956. Unmarked. Original colorful box marked P-815.*

178. VIRGA 'PLAY-MATES' NURSE

8". *Hard plastic head that turns when walked, blue sleep eyes, closed mouth, light-brown wig, five-piece hard plastic, child body. Original cotton white dress, blue felt cape, vinyl cap. Circa 1956. Unmarked. Original box marked P-816.*

179. THREE VIRGA HI-HEEL TEEN FASHIONS

Three packaged fashions for 8 1/2" teen doll include pink formal gown with multi-colored bodice, pink nylon dinner dress and blue formal gown.

180. THREE VIRGA PLAY-MATE FASHIONS

Three packaged fashions for 8" child doll include cotton nurse uniform, red felt coat, pant and hat set, yellow party dress with panty, ribbon and puppet.

181. THREE VIRGA PLAY-MATE FASHIONS

Three packaged fashions for 8" child doll include white bride gown with veil, nurse uniform and pink bridesmaid dress with veil.

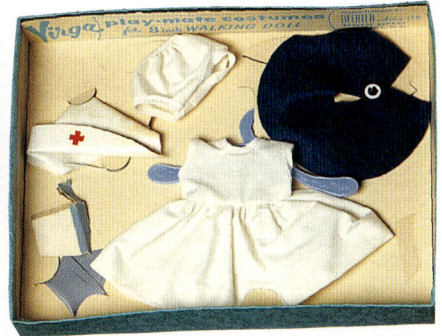

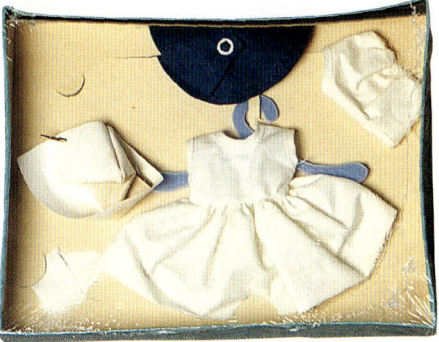

182. AMERICAN CHARACTER 'SWEET SUE' BRIDE

30". Hard plastic head, green sleep eyes, closed mouth, blonde rooted wig, five-piece (jointed knees) hard plastic child body, two-piece vinyl arms. Original white satin, lace, ribbon and tulle gown with pearl accents, veil, and pantaloons. Circa 1952. Marked American Character on head. Original labeled box.

183. 'MARY-LU WALKER' IN BOX

17 1/2". Hard plastic head that turns when walked, blue sleep eyes, open mouth with four teeth, felt tongue, blonde wig, five-piece hard plastic child body. Original red dress with plaid collar, cuffs and waist, original brown box and wrist tag. Circa 1955. Unmarked.

184. A & H DOLL 'GIGI' WALKER

7 1/2". Hard plastic head that turns when walked, blue sleep eyes, closed mouth, brown wig, five-piece hard plastic child body. Original red vinyl raincoat, red boots and panty. Circa 1955. Unmarked. Original fashion brochure and decorated box.

185. A & H DOLL 'GIGI' WALKER

7 1/2". Hard plastic head that turns when walked, blue sleep eyes, closed mouth, brown wig, five-piece hard plastic child body. Original pink gown brushed with gold, pink net wrap, gold shoes. Circa 1955. Unmarked. Original fashion brochure and box.

186. GIGI BOXED FASHION

Original outfit for 7 1/2" doll includes red skating dress of felt and nylon, panty, cap and skates. Original box #724.

187. IDEAL SAUCY WALKER

22". Hard plastic head, blue flirty sleep eyes, open mouth with two teeth and molded tongue, brown wig, five-piece hard plastic child body. Original cotton polka-dot dress with fragile organdy inserts, original wrist tags and box. Circa 1952. Marked Ideal Doll on head and back.

188. IDEAL SAUCY WALKER

22". Hard plastic head, blue flirty sleep eyes, open mouth with two teeth and molded tongue, brown wig, five-piece hard plastic, child body. Original cotton diamond-print dress with organdy insert and sleeves, original wrist tags and box. Circa 1952. Marked Ideal Doll on head and back.

189. DELUXE 'SWEET ROSEMARY'

30". Vinyl head, blue sleep eyes, closed mouth, blonde rooted hair, unusual one-piece vinyl adult body. Original pink nylon and tulle gown with silver accents, matching mitts, pearl earrings, hair clip and necklace, pink purse and heels. Circa 1957-60. Marked 152 on head. Original box with colorful description.

190. HASBRO BRIDAL PARTY SEWING KIT

Unusual set of four hard plastic dolls semi-dressed in different colored gowns for a wedding. Supplies you with thread, needles, ribbon and material to finish sewing the dresses needed to create the wedding party. Circa 1955. Original colorful box.

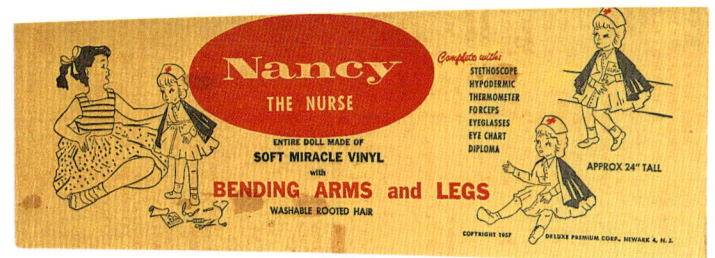
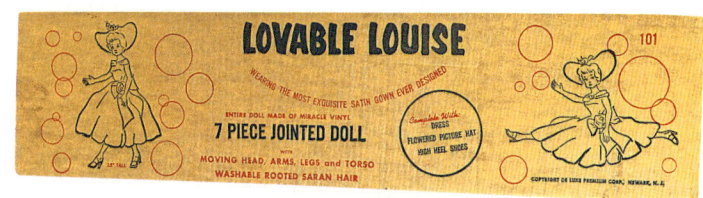

191. DELUXE 'NANCY THE NURSE'

23". Vinyl head, green sleep eyes, closed mouth, rooted blonde hair, one-piece bendable vinyl body. Original cotton nurse's uniform with cape and hat, additional envelope of medical accessories and diploma. Circa 1957. Marked AE 554.

192. DELUXE 'LOVABLE LOUISE'

24". Vinyl head, blue sleep eyes, closed mouth, rooted blonde hair, six-piece (swivel waist) hard plastic adult body. Original pink and purple satin dress with large matching hat, heels. Circa 1957. Marked 11 on head. Original brochure and descriptive box.

193. ELITE 'VICKI' THE WALKING DOLL

8". Hard plastic head that turns when walked, blue sleep eyes, closed mouth, braided auburn wig, five-piece hard plastic child body. Original green and white waffle cotton with matching sunhat. Circa 1955. Unmarked. Original box marked "Alice".

194. ELITE 'VICKI' MAJORETTE

8". Hard plastic head that turns when walked, closed mouth, blonde wig, five-piece hard plastic child body. Original white flannel, gold trim majorette uniform with hat, baton and boots. Circa 1955. Original box.

195. FIVE BOXED VICKI FASHIONS

Five outfits in original packages includes gold lounging pajamas with glasses, two nurse's uniforms with cape, cap and bag, bathing suit with parasol, glasses and sunhat, majorette uniform with hat and baton. Circa 1955.

196. LITTLE DARLING 'KATHI' DOLL

12". Vinyl head, blue sleep eyes, closed mouth, blonde rooted hair, five-piece hard vinyl child body. Original red felt coat and hat with faux leopard collar and cuffs. Circa 1959. Unmarked.

197. LITTLE DARLING 'KATHI' DOLL

12". Vinyl head, blue sleep eyes, closed mouth, blonde rooted hair, five-piece hard vinyl child body. Original blue felt coat and hat with faux leopard collar and cuffs. Circa 1959. Unmarked.

198. LITTLE DARLING 'KATHI' DOLL

12". Vinyl head, blue sleep eyes, closed mouth, blonde rooted hair, five-piece hard vinyl child body. Original pink felt coat and hat with faux leopard collar and cuffs. Circa 1959. Unmarked.

199. DELUXE 'BETTY THE BEAUTIFUL BRIDE'

29". Vinyl head, blue sleep eyes, closed mouth, brown rooted hair, one-piece rubber body. Original satin and net gown with veil, bouquet, wrist tag, wall plaque and recording of Bing Crosby's "Because". Circa 1957-1959. Marked 251 AE 7 on back of head.

200. DELUXE 'SWEET AMY SCHOOL GIRL' DOLL

25". Vinyl head, blue sleep eyes, closed mouth, rooted blonde hair, one-piece rubber body. Original red cotton shirt with blue kiltie jumper. Accessories include school bag, books, blackboard, eraser, chalk, jigsaw puzzle and American flag. Circa 1957. Marked A1 on head. Original box and tag included.

201. HORSMAN 'POOR PITIFUL PEARL'

17". Vinyl head, black sleep eyes, closed thin mouth, rooted blonde hair, five-piece hard plastic child body. Original calico "rag" dress with head scarf, hose and shoes. Original box and play booklet. Circa 1963. Marked 1963 Wm Steig Horsman Dolls Inc.

202. HORSMAN 'POOR PITIFUL PEARL'

12". Vinyl head, grey sleep eyes, closed thin mouth, rooted blonde hair, five-piece hard plastic child body. Original calico "rags" dress with head scarf, hose, shoes and pink party dress with white socks and shoes. Original box and booklet. Circa 1963. Marked Horsman Dolls Inc 1963 Wm Steig P11 5 on head.

203. LIBBY 'I DREAM OF JEANNIE' DOLL

19". Vinyl head, blue sleep eyes, closed mouth, rooted blonde frosted hair, five-piece hard plastic adult body. Original red felt and pink chiffon, two-piece Arabian outfit. Circa 1965.

Marked 8 1965 Libby on head.

204. BETSY McCALL FASHION

Style #8202 "On the Ice" skating outfit includes red knit top, white felt skirt and hat, panty and ice skates.

205. IDEAL 'THUMBELINA' BABY

18". Vinyl head, painted features, rooted blonde hair, vinyl baby limbs on cloth body. Original tagged blue cotton dress and panty, instructions for working the motion mechanism in her back (it works). Circa 1961. Marked Ideal Doll GTT-10 on head. Original picture box.

206. MATTEL 'CHATTY CATHY'

20". Vinyl head, brown sleep eyes, open mouth with two teeth, freckles, rooted short brown hair, five-piece hard plastic child body with grill, pull-string at neck (mute). Tagged red cotton playsuit with apron overlay, red coat with collar. Circa 1960. Marked Chatty Cathy TM, Patents Pending MCMLX By Mattel Inc Hawthorne Calif.

207. MATTEL 'CHATTY BABY'

18". Hard plastic head, blue sleep eyes, open mouth with two teeth, rooted blonde hair (fuzzy), five-piece hard plastic toddler body with stomach grill, pull-string missing from neck. Original red cotton playsuit with apron, bib, hat and booties. Circa 1961. Marked with patent number, foreign pats. pending.

208. MATTEL 'TINY CHATTY BABY'

15". Hard plastic head, blue sleep eyes, open mouth with two teeth, rooted blonde hair, five-piece hard plastic toddler body with stomach grill, pull-string at back of neck (mute). Tagged original blue playsuit with bib, blue overcoat, booties. Circa 1962. Marked C 1962 Mattel Inc Hawthorne Calif.

209. MATTEL BLACK 'CHATTY BABY'

17". Hard plastic head, brown sleep eyes, open mouth with two teeth, rooted black hair, five-piece hard plastic toddler body with stomach grill, pull-string at back of neck (mute). Tagged white cotton playsuit with red apron, bib and booties. Circa 1961. Marked with patent number, foreign pats. pending.

210. MATTEL BLACK 'CHATTY CATHY'

19". Hard plastic head, brown sleep eyes, open mouth with two teeth, rooted black short hair, five-piece hard plastic child body with stomach grill, no pull-ring at back of neck. Tagged original pink and white dress with eyelet pinafore, red velvet coat, matching hat. Circa 1963. Marked with copyright, patent number, etc.

211. MATTEL CHATTY BABY PLAYTIME OUTFITS

Three packaged outfits for Chatty Baby include #342 Sleeper Set, #344 Terry Playsuit and #343 Pink Coverall Set.

212. MATTEL "CHARMIN' CHATTY"

24". Vinyl head, side-glancing blue sleep eyes, thin smile, rooted auburn hair, five-piece hard plastic child body with elongated legs, grill in stomach, pull-ring at back of neck (her voice works). Original cotton nautical skirt and top, red socks, saddle shoes. Original box and hang tag. Circa 1961. Marked C 1961 Mattel Inc, Hawthorne Calif USA.

213. MATTEL 'CHATTY CATHY' WITH BOX

20". Vinyl head, brown sleep eyes, freckles, open mouth with two teeth, rooted brown hair, five-piece hard plastic child body, grill in stomach and pull-ring at back of neck (she talks). Original pink striped dress with eyelet pinafore. Original wrist tag and box. Circa 1960. Marked MCMLX Patents Pending. Included is Chatty Cathy outfit #695 Nursery School in original package.

214. MATTEL 'TINY CHATTY BROTHER' IN BOX

15". Hard vinyl head, blue sleep eyes, open mouth with two teeth, blonde rooted hair, five-piece hard plastic toddler body, grill in stomach, pull-ring at back of neck (mute). Original blue playsuit with name, matching cap and booties. Circa 1962. Marked C 1962 Mattel Inc Hawthorne Calif USA.

215. MATTEL CHARMIN' CHATTY OUTFIT

#367 "Let's Play Nurse" uniform includes top, pants, stethoscope, slippers, needle, bracelet, health certificate and booklet with record.

216. #297 "Let's Play Birthday Party"
includes red and white party dress, vinyl shoes, crepe paper, cake, candles, card with envelope, booklet and record.

217. #362 "Let's Play Cinderella"
includes pink nylon dress with net skirt, cape, rag dress, "glass" slippers, broom, magic wand, booklet and record.

218. TINY CHATTY BABY COVER AND PILLOW SET

Original packaged white nylon pillow and cover with Chatty Baby picture. Made by Newark Comfort Company.

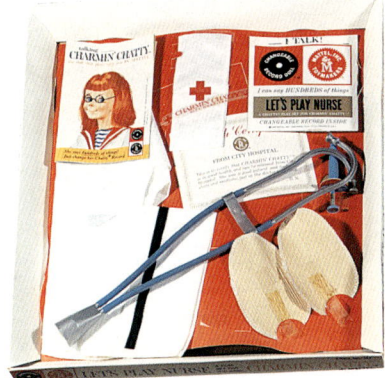

BARBIE AND FAMILY

219. MATTEL #1 BARBIE

11 1/2". Blonde back braid, curly bangs, painted irises, arched brows, red lip and nail coloring. 1959. Original black and white suit, black open-toe #1 heels, wrapped booklet and sunglasses. Original box. #2 stand.

220. MATTEL #3 DRESSED DISPLAY DOLL #864

11 1/2". Blonde ponytail, curly bangs, brown liner over eyes, red lips. 1960. Wearing #964 "Gay Parisienne" outfit. Pink and white box has stand included. See label close-up.

221. 1959 EASTER PARADE #971

Includes dress, coat, hat, gloves, necklace, earrings and shoes (no purse).

222. 1959 GAY PARISIENNE #964

Includes dress, stole, gloves, purse, hat, earrings, and necklace.

223. 1959 ROMAN HOLIDAY #968

Includes striped coat, dress, compact, gloves, glasses, comb, necklace, missing hat, eyeglass case and belt.

224. PLANTATION BELLE #966

Includes dress, petticoat, hat, purse, gloves, bracelet, necklace, 1 pink earring, shoes.

225. BARBIE PURSE FASHION PAK

Three assorted purses in original packaging. 1962-1963.

Box label of Lot #220.

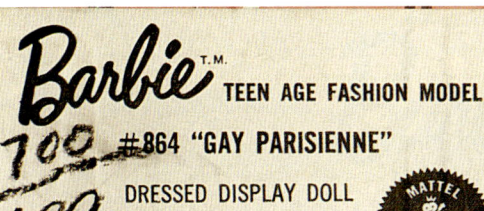

226. MATTEL #5 BARBIE

11 1/2". Blonde ponytail, firmly-textured bangs, teal eyeliner, red lips and nail coloring, original swimsuit, pearl earrings (slight ear green). 1961. Original box, stand and wrapped booklet with sunglasses and shoes.

227. MATTEL #6 BARBIE

11 1/2". Auburn ponytail, firmly-textured hair, rich coloring of eyes and nails, coral lips, original swimsuit, golden pearl earrings and shoes. 1962. Original box, stand and booklet.

228. MATTEL #6 BARBIE

11 1/2". Ash-blonde ponytail, firmly-textured hair, rich coloring of eyes and nails, coral lips, original swimsuit, pearl earrings (slight green). Original box, stand, wrapped booklet with shoes and wrist tag.

229. MATTEL BUBBLE CUT BARBIE

11 1/2". Auburn hair, delicate painting of eyes, full pink lips, decorated nails, original swimsuit, pearl earrings (slight green). 1962. Original box, stand, wrist tag and wrapped booklet with shoes.

230. MATTEL BUBBLE CUT BARBIE

11 1/2". Light-brown hair, vivid coloring of eyes with shadowing, rich red decoration of lips and nails. 1961. Dressed in #961 "Evening Splendour" outfit with large pearl earrings (slight ear green). Original early box, booklet and stand.

231. MATTEL SWIRL PONYTAIL BARBIE

11 1/2". Platinum-blonde hair with original ribbon and hairpin, rich coloring of eyes and nails, peach lips, original swimsuit, pearl earrings and shoes. 1964. Original box and booklet.

232. MATTEL FASHION QUEEN BARBIE

11 1/2". Brown molded hair, pale blue eyeliner, pink lips, pearl earrings (slight ear green), original gold and white striped swimsuit and head wrap. Includes wig stand with three wigs, booklet, stand and wrist tag.

233. MATTEL TRADE-IN BARBIE

11 1/2". Brunette hair, blue eyes with rooted lashes, pink lips and blush, original orange hair ribbon, orange vinyl two-piece suit with fish-net cover-up, twist 'n turn waist, bendable legs, booklet, wrist bracelet and original plastic bag.

234. KNITTING FOR BARBIE KIT

Kit #8014 includes wool, needles and instructions to make a coat and hat for Barbie. 1962. Tin cylinder with pictures of outfits on back.

235. GERMAN BILD LILLI

7". Hard plastic body, painted and detailed face, blonde hair in ponytail, original swimsuit, molded earrings and shoes, stand with name and circular paper label with patent numbers. Circa 1960. Original plastic circular tube holds this hard-to-find petite size.

BARBIE FASHIONS
never removed from package

236. RESORT SET #963, *knit top, shorts, jacket, visor, bracelet, shoes and booklet.*

237. WINTER HOLIDAY SET #975, *knit hooded sweatshirt, jacket with belt, gloves, tights, carry bag, shoes and booklet.*

238. PEACHY-FLEECY COAT #915, *coat, hat, gloves, purse, shoes and booklet.*

239. MOOD FOR MUSIC #940, *knit halter, sweater, pants, shoes, necklace (broken) and booklet.*

240. AFTER FIVE #934, *dress, hat, shoes and booklet.*

241. COMMUTER SET #916, *white satin and blue check blouses, navy knit suit, hat, gloves, necklace, hatbox, shoes and booklet.*

242. ICE BREAKER #942, *bodysuit, jacket, skirt, hose, skates and booklet.*

243. EVENING SPLENDOUR #961, *gold dress, matching coat, hat, purse, necklace, gloves, hankie, shoes and booklet.*

244. BARBIE AND SKIPPER PAPER DOLLS

Whitman #1957, two stand-up dolls, six pages of costumes. Uncut, excellent condition. Circa 1964.

245. SWEATER GIRL #976, knit sweater and shell, skirt, book, bowl with yarn and "needles", scissors, shoes and booklet.

246. WINTER WOW #1486, jacket, skirt, lame boots, muff, hat, hanger and booklet.

247. LET'S DANCE #978, dress, purse, necklace, shoes and booklet.

248. FRIDAY NITE DATE #979, dress, jumper, tray with drinks, shoes and booklet.

249. REGISTERED NURSE #991, uniform dress, cape, hat, eyeglasses, diploma, medicine bottle, spoon, water bottle, shoes and booklet.

250. MATTEL MIDGE

11 1/2". Titian hair, rich eye, lips and nail coloring, coral lips, original two-piece swimsuit. 1963. Original box, wrapped booklet with shoes, stand and wrist tag.

251. MATTEL #1 KEN

12". Brunette flocked hair, brown eyeliner, turquoise eyes, mauve lips, original swim trunks and jacket. 1961. Original box, stand, wrapped booklet with sandals and wrist tag.

252. MATTEL #1 KEN

12". Blonde flocked hair, turquoise eyes, dark lips, original swim trunks and jacket. 1961. Original box, stand, wrapped booklet with sandals and wrist tag.

253. MATTEL #2 KEN

12". Blonde molded hair, bright blue eyes with brown liner, pale peach lips, original swim trunk and jacket. 1963. Original box, stand, wrapped booklet with sandals and wrist tag.

254. MATTEL #1 KEN IN COSTUME

12". Blonde flocked hair, brown liner and brows, turquoise eyes, wearing #772 "The Prince" costume (missing stone from cap). 1961. Original box and stand.

255. MATTEL #1 KEN IN OUTFIT

12". Brunette flocked hair, brown liner and brows, turquoise eyes, pink lips, wearing #785 "Dreamboat" outfit. 1961. Original box, wrist tag and stand.

KEN OUTFITS
never removed from packages

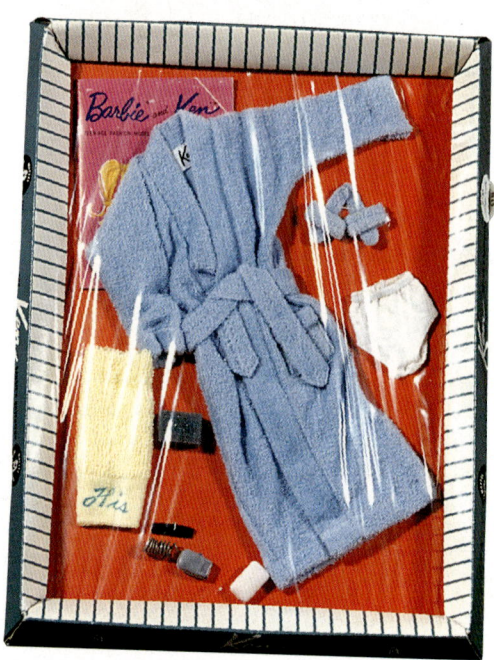

256. CASUALS #782, knit shirt, pants, cap, socks, car keys, shoes and booklet.

257. SPORT SHORTS #783, casual print shirt, shorts, knee socks, shoes and booklet.

258. TERRY TOGS #784, terry bathrobe, slippers, briefs, towel, comb, razor, soap, sponge and booklet.

259. RALLY DAY #788, beige car coat, cap, road map, car keys and booklet.

260. SATURDAY DATE #786, white shirt, grey jacket and pants, tie, socks, shoes and booklet.

261. TUXEDO #787, black jacket and pants, shirt, cummerbund, bow tie, corsage, socks, shoes and booklet.

262. MATTEL STRAIGHT LEG SKIPPER

9". Blonde hair, blue eyes, pink lips, wearing #1904 "Flower Girl" outfit with #1900 "Under-Pretties". 1964. Original box, swimsuit, stand, wrist tag and set of curlers, brush, comb and mirror.

263. MATTEL STRAIGHT LEG SKIPPER IN FASHION /pink

9". Red hair, blue eyes, pink lips, wearing #1907 "School Days" outfit. 1964. Original box, swimsuit, stand, wrist tag, and wrapped booklet with flats, comb and brush included.

264. MATTEL STRAIGHT LEG SKIPPER IN FASHION

9". Unusual streaked brown hair, blue eyes, pink lips, tan complexion, wearing #1922 green "Town Togs" outfit. 1964. Original box, swimsuit, stand, wrist tag and wrapped booklet with flats, comb and brush included.

265. MATTEL STRAIGHT LEG SKIPPER

9". Blonde hair, blue side-glancing eyes with brown liner, pink lips, original red and white swimsuit. 1964. Original box, stand, headwrap, wrapped booklet with shoes, comb and brush.

266. MATTEL STRAIGHT LEG SKOOTER

9". Brunette hair in pigtails, brown eyes with black liner, freckles, pink lips, wearing #1935 "Learning to Ride" outfit. 1965. Original box, two-piece swimsuit, stand, wrapped booklet with shoes, comb and brush.

267. MATTEL STRAIGHT LEG SKOOTER

9". Red hair in pigtails, brown eyes with black liner, freckles, pink lips, wearing #1936 "Sledding Fun" outfit. 1965. Original box, plastic sled.

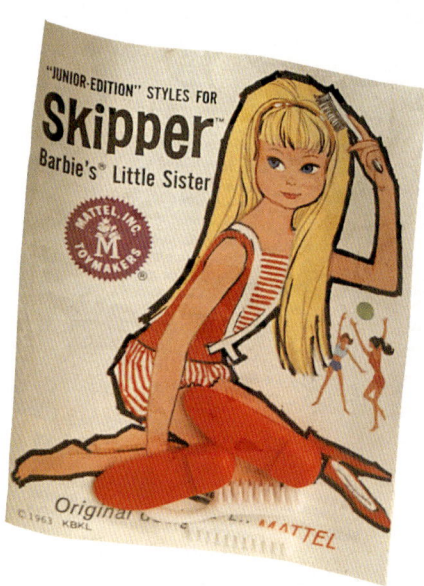

268. MATTEL STRAIGHT LEG SKOOTER

9". Pale blonde hair in pigtails, brown eyes with black liner, freckles, pink lips, wearing #1928 "Rainy Day Checkers" outfit. 1965. Original box, two-piece swimsuit, stand and brush.

269A. MATTEL RICKY

9". Red molded hair, blue eyes with black liner, freckles, pink lips, swim trunks with jacket. 1965. Original box, stand and wrist tag.

269B. MATTEL RICKY

9". Red molded hair, blue eyes with heavy black liner, freckles, light peach lips, tan complexion, wearing #1502 "Saturday Show" outfit. 1965. Original box, swim trunks and jacket.

RICKY OUTFITS
never removed from packages

270. LIGHTS OUT #1501, *terry bathrobe, pajamas, slippers and booklet.*

271. LET'S EXPLORE #1506, *plaid jacket, pants, socks, sneakers and booklet.*

272. SKATEBOARD SET #1505, *striped top, shorts, socks, skateboard, sneakers and booklet.*

273. SUNDAY SUIT #1503, *striped jacket, white shirt, black pants, red socks, black shoes and booklet.*

274. LITTLE LEAGUER #1504, *knit shirt, jeans, red socks, baseball cap, fielder's glove, baseball, sneakers and booklet.*

275. MEN-MY-DOLL #1913, *pink gingham dress, pink slip, small Barbie doll with matching skirt, socks, flats and booklet.*

276. DREAMTIME #1909, *two-piece pajamas, robe, felt cat, slippers, phone, phone directory and booklet.*

277. SILK 'N FANCY #1902, *dress, belt, socks, flats and booklet.*

278. RED SENSATION #1901, *dress, hat, gloves, socks, flats and booklet.*

279. BALLET CLASS #1905, *leotard, tights, pink tutu, program, floral headpiece, slippers, bag and booklet.*

280. MASQUERADE PARTY #1903, *costume dress, panty, hat, mask, invitation, flats with pom-poms and booklet.*

281. SUNNY PASTELS #1910, *multi-color dress, matching bag, socks, flats and booklet.*

282. SKATING FUN #1908, *white and red unitard, skirt, muff, hat, skates and booklet.*

283. DAY AT THE FAIR #1911, *top, headscarf, wrap skirt, small Barbie doll, flats and booklet.*

284. COOKIE TIME #1912, *dress with belt, recipe book, cookie mix, rolling pin, bowl, spoon, flats and booklet.*

285. SCHOOL DAYS #1907, *pink sweater, skirt, shirt, knee socks, bowl of yarn and needles, flats and booklet.*

286. PLATTER PARTY #1914, *formal dress with pom-pom trim, record player with two records, flats and booklet.*

287. **OUTDOOR CASUALS #1915**, *knit sweater, dickey, pants, gloves, yo-yo, flats and booklet.*

288. **SCHOOL GIRL #1921**, *pleated top, skirt, jacket, hat, eyeglasses, books with strap, apple, socks, flats and booklet.*

289. **SHIP AHOY! #1918**, *dress, nautical vest, camera, toy boat, two travel brochures, socks, flats and booklet.*

290. **RAIN OR SHINE! #1916**, *raincoat, cap, umbrella, boots and booklet.*

291. **CHILL CHASER #1926**, *fuzzy coat, beret, socks, flats and booklet.*

292. **CAN YOU PLAY? #1923**, *play dress, scarf, panty, ball, flats and booklet.*

293. **LAND AND SEA #1917**, *knit striped top, jacket, pedal pushers, cap, sunglasses, flats and booklet.*

294. **FUNTIME #1920**, *pants, sport shirt, embroidered top, jacket, croquet mallet, stick, ball and wicket, flats and booklet.* tulips, Birds

295. **HAPPY BIRTHDAY #1919**, *party dress, slip, hat, cake with candles, doily, invitation, napkins and noise crackers, present, gloves, socks, flats and booklet.*

296. **COUNTRY PICNIC #1933**, *dress with matching bag, picnic blanket, napkin, ball, butterfly net with butterfly, glass, ice cream cone, thermos, plate with watermelon slice, hamburger, fork with hot dog, flats and booklet.* Butterflies

297. **GLAD PLAIDS** #1946, top, skirt, coat, purse, cap, lace hose, ankle boots and booklet.

298. **LEARNING TO RIDE** #1935, riding jacket and jodhpurs, top, gloves, crop, hat, boots and booklet.

299. **JUNIOR BRIDESMAID** #1934, pink formal gown, matching tulle hat, gloves, basket with flowers, socks, flats and booklet.

300. **HOPSCOTCHINS** #1968, striped jacket, shorts, hanger, flats and booklet.

301. **KNIT BIT** #1969, knit dress, hat, shorts, knee socks, hanger, jump rope, ice cream sundae, ankle boots and booklet.

302. **FLOWER SHOWERS** #1939, plastic raincoat, matching hat, hanger, boots and booklet.

303. **ALL SPRUCED UP** #1941, tweed dress, lace hose, purse, hat, hanger, flats and booklet.

304. **RIGHT IN STYLE** #1942, floral dress, green shift, hat, granny glasses, hanger, socks, flats and booklet.

305. **TRIM TWOSOME** #1960, dress, purse, jacket, hanger, flats and booklet.

306. **LOLAPALOOZAS** #1947, midriff top, jacket, bell bottoms, full top, shorts, skirt, hanger, flats and booklet.

307. PINK PRINCESS #1747, dress, coat, hose, hat, hanger, flats and booklet.

308. DAISY CRAZY #1732, dress, knee socks, hanger, flats and booklet.

309. VELVET BLUSH #1737, dress, coat, gloves, socks, flats and booklet.

310. WOOLY WINNER #1746, plaidskirt/red knit dress, wooly coat, hat, knee socks, purse, hanger, ankle boots and booklet.

311. TENNIS TIME #3466, tennis dress, socks, hanger, racquet, ball flats and booklet.

312. CHILLY CHUMS #1973, pink lime green dress, coat, hat, hanger, stockings, flats and booklet.

313. ACTION FASHION ACCESSORY PAK

Includes flats, ice skates, boots, jump rope, tennis ball, radio and sunglasses.

314. BALLERINA #3471, blue satin tutu, hose, hanger, slippers, shoe bag and booklet. blue + yellow

315. ALL OVER FELT #3476, felt dress, coat, hat, bag, hose, flats and booklet. Blue

316. MATTEL TUTTI "WALKIN' MY DOLLY" SET

Set #3552 comes sealed with 6" blonde, bendable Tutti in red and white dot playsuit and hat, plastic carriage with small rubber doll, comb and brush set and booklet. 1966.

317. MATTEL TUTTI 'MELODY IN PINK' SET

Set #3555 comes sealed with 6" blonde, bendable Tutti in pink nylon and dotted tulle dress, seated with plastic baby grand piano, comb, brush set and booklet included. 1966.

318. MATTEL TODD

6". Cinnamon-hair, brown eyes, watermelon smile, all-vinyl and bendable, mint in original sealed package. 1967.

319. MATTEL 'FLORENCE NIDDLE' KIDDLE SET

Liddle Kiddles set #3507 with 3" bendable doll with rooted hair in nurse uniform with plastic baby, blanket, carriage, comb and brush set and storybook. 1966.

320. MATTEL TUTTI PLAY CASE

Pink vinyl case with clear center panel for doll to stand, pictures of Tutti on front. Blonde, bendable, Tutti doll included in original floral print dress and shoes.

321. MATTEL TUTTI PLAY CASE

Orange floral vinyl case with clear panel to side for doll, closet inside with hangers, turquoise brush set. Brunette, bendable Tutti doll included in original pink gingham sundress with hat and shoes.

TUTTI OUTFITS
never removed from package

322. LET'S PLAY BARBIE #3608, dress, panty, hairband, socks, small plastic Barbie doll with red carry case, shoes and booklet.

323. SEA SHORE SHORTIES #3614, dress, two-piece bathing suit, toy boat, beach ball, shoes and booklet.

324. PINKY PJ'S #3616, two-piece pajamas, baby doll with blanket, slippers, comb and brush set and booklet.

325. CLOWNING AROUND #3606, dress, panty, cloth clown doll, shoes and booklet.

PAPER DOLLS

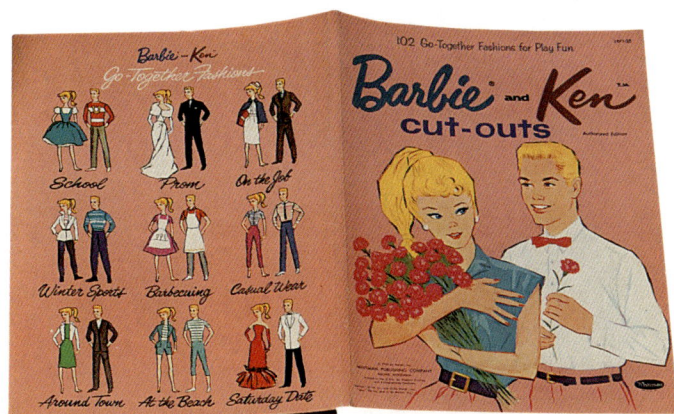

326. FRANCIE CARRYING CASE

Six-sided vinyl carrying case for Francie and clothing, decorated with three color illustrations of Francie in various fashions. 1965.

327. BARBIE AND KEN #1971/59 Whitman, 1962. *Fold-out portfolio with 102 fashions. Uncut, excellent condition.*

328. BARBIE DOLL #1963 Whitman, 1962. *Features Bubble-cut Barbie with many fashions. Doll and some clothes cut.*

329. BARBIE AND KEN #1976/59 Whitman, 1963. *Barbie and Ken with fashions and small car. Cut.*

330. BARBIE, KEN AND MIDGE #1976/59 Whitman, 1963. *With 6 pages of fashions. Uncut.*

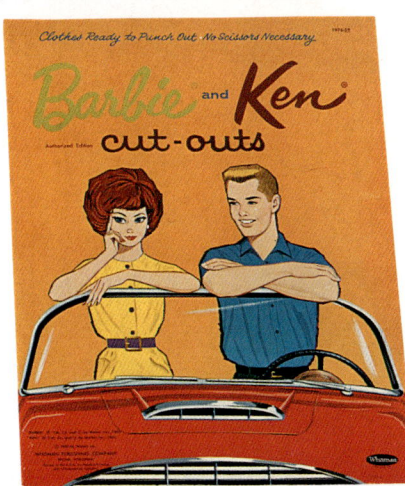

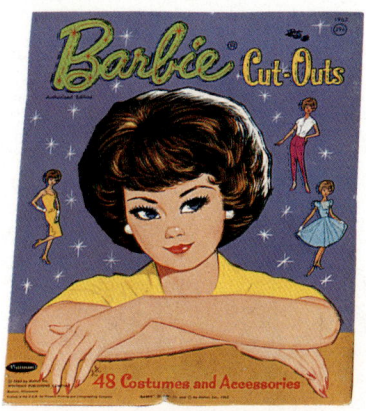

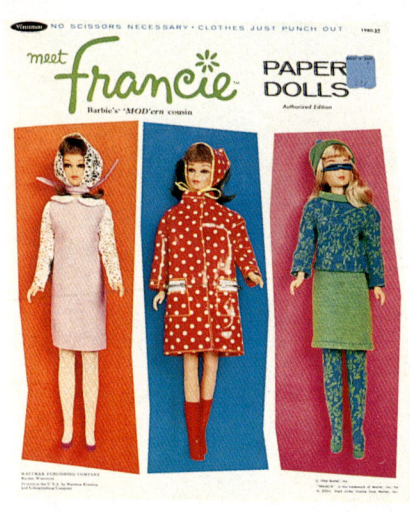
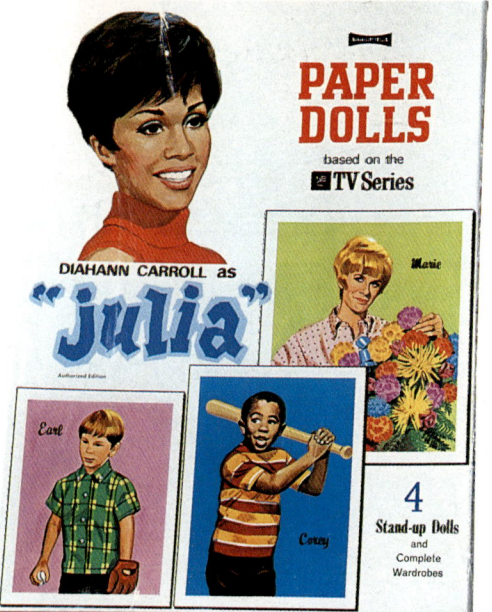

331. BARBIE #1962 Whitman, 1963. 6 pages of fashions. Uncut.

332. BARBIE COSTUME DOLLS #1976/59 Whitman. Barbie, Ken, Midge, Allan and Skipper with costumes and three scenery backgrounds. Uncut.

333. MIDGE #1962 Whitman, 1963. Redhead and blonde Midges with 6 pages of fashions. Uncut.

334. MEET FRANCIE #1980/59 Whitman, 1966. Blonde and brunette Francies with 6 pages of mod fashions. Uncut.

335. JULIA #6055 Saalfield, 1968. Unopened box of 4 dolls with complete wardrobes.

336. TAMMY #1997/59 Whitman, 1964. Tammy, Ted, Pepper, Mom and Dad with 6 pages of fashions. Uncut.

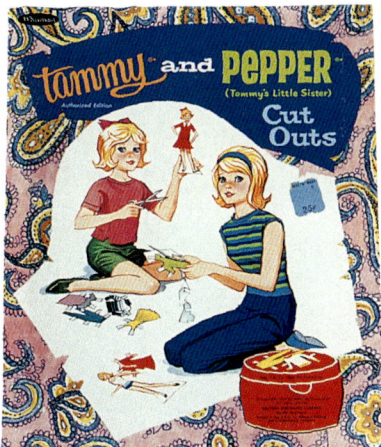
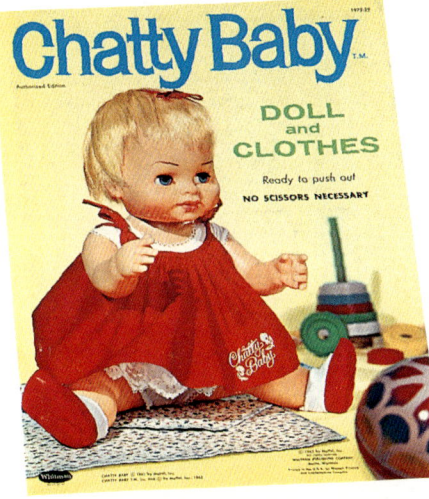

337. TAMMY #1885D Watkins/Strathmore, 1963. Blonde and redhead Tammy with 8 pages of fashions. Uncut.

338. TAMMY AND PEPPER #1953 Whitman, 1966. Dolls with 6 pages of fashions. Uncut.

339. CHATTY BABY #1972/59 Whitman, 1963. Chatty Baby and assorted cut play clothes.

340. TINY CHATTY TWINS #1985/59 Whitman, 1963. Adorable twins with 6 pages of clothes. Uncut.

341. CHATTY CATHY #1961 Whitman, 1963. Tote bag with doll and 45 costumes and accessories. Uncut.

342. CHARMIN' CHATTY #1985/59 Whitman, 1964. Doll with passport, international wardrobe and travel case. Uncut.

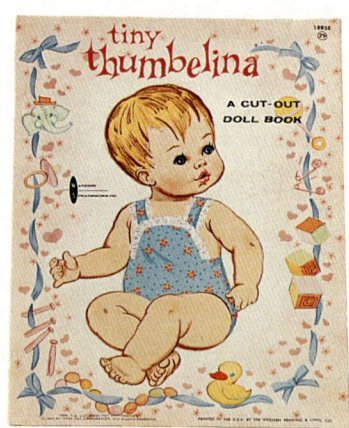
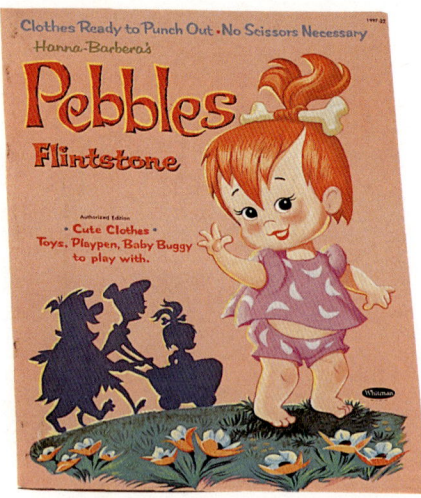

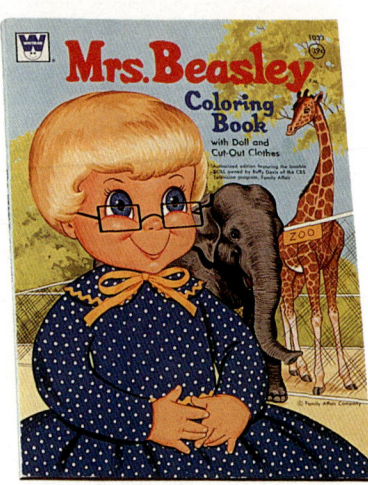

343. POLLYANA #GF163 Golden Press, 1960. *Fashions, friends and wardrobe. Uncut.*

344. TINY THUMBELINA #1885E Watkins/Strathmore, 1963. *Two dolls with assorted clothing. Uncut.*

345. PEBBLES #1997/59 Whitman, 1963. *Punch-out clothing with accessories. Uncut.*

346. KISSY #1337 Saalfield, 1963. *Unusual two-piece doll reaches 16" when joined together. Uncut with assorted dresses.*

347. BUFFY #1995/69 Whitman, 1968. *Doll with clothes and Mrs. Beasley doll with crib. Uncut.*

348. MRS. BEASLEY COLORING BOOK #1033 Whitman, 1969. *Cut-out doll on back cover, fashions to color.*

349. BETSY McCALL #5130 Saalfield, 1965. Doll, friends and wardrobe.

350. SHIRLEY TEMPLE #5110 Saalfield, 1963. Features 18" fold-up doll with easel to stand, uncut fashions.

351. SHIRLEY TEMPLE #4435 Saalfield, 1963. Two dolls with pages of fashions. Uncut.

352. MARY HARTLINE #210425 Whitman, 1952. Two dolls with pages to color and cut-out.

353. MARY HARTLINE #1175/15 Whitman, 1953. Two dolls with assorted fashions. Uncut.

354. NATIONAL VELVET #1948 Whitman, 1962. Doll and assorted riding gear and fashions. Uncut.

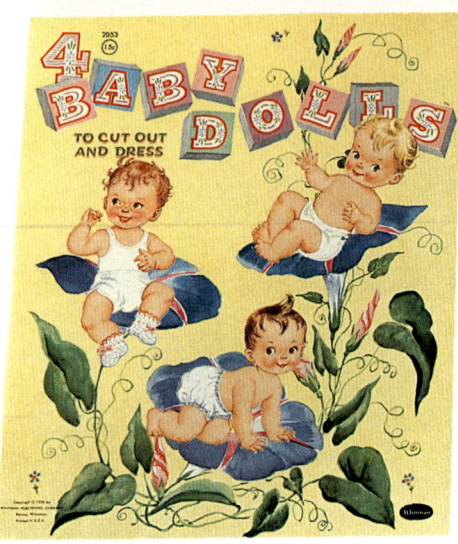 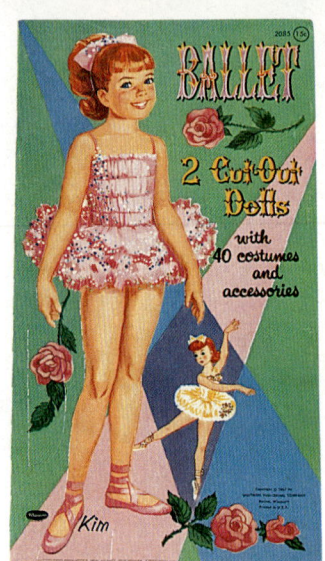 

355. LUCY LOCKET/KITTY FISHER #1565 Merrill, 1956. Charming dolls, pets and outfits. Uncut.

356. FAIRY PRINCESSES #1548 Merrill, 1956. Meg, Kim, Pam and Peter dolls with outfits. Uncut.

357. A DAY WITH DIANE #1770 Saalfield, 1957. Diane, Peggy and Carol cut-outs with clothing. Uncut.

358. 4 BABY DOLLS #2053 Whitman, 1958. Babies, pets and toys with many outfits. Uncut.

359. BALLET #2085 Whitman, 1961. Kim and Pam with assorted ballet costumes and outfits. Uncut.

360. 6 AND SWEET 16 #2582 Merrill, 1955. Three sets of big and little sisters with clothing and pets. Uncut.

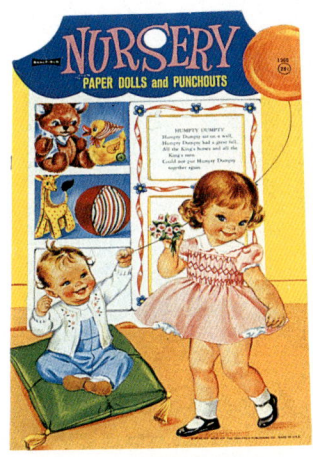

361. SPORTS TIME #2090 Whitman, 1952. Toddler with assorted play outfits, fold-up picnic basket on back cover. Uncut.

362. NURSERY PAPER DOLLS #1368 Saalfield, 1958. Three toddlers with clothing and toys. Uncut.

363. FLOWER GIRLS #4431 Saalfield, 1957. Brenda and Phyllis with carry case and many outfits. Uncut.

364. HERE IS SUSIE/JOANN #1560 Merrill, 1962. Two girls with wardrobe. Uncut.

365. SEVEN CHILDREN LIVE IN A SHOE #2572 Merrill, 1958. Children with assorted clothing. Uncut.

366. BETTY BLUE AND PATTY PINK #2570 Merrill, 1958. With wrap-around dresses. Uncut.

367. BABY GROWS UP #1978/59 Whitman, 1950. Inventive set with 4 dolls at varying ages, baby book, birth certificate, photo album and complete layette. Uncut.

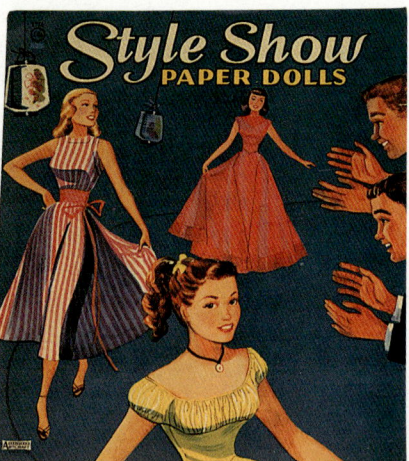

368. THE HEAVENLY BLUE WEDDING #2580 Merrill, 1955. Six bridal party dolls and clothing. Uncut.

369. STYLE SHOE PAPER DOLLS #1725 Saalfield, 1953. Three cut-out girls with fashions. Uncut.

370. THE STORY PRINCESS #2761 Saalfield, 1952. Three Arlene Dalton dolls with fashions. Uncut.

371. PRETTY AS A PICTURE #2772 Saalfield, 1953. Two lovely dolls with glamorous gowns. Uncut.

372. THE WEDDING #1988/100 Whitman, 1960. Playbook includes bridal party dolls with full range of clothing, three-section book with each page set being a different setting to display the dolls. Uncut.